Gerald Scarfe

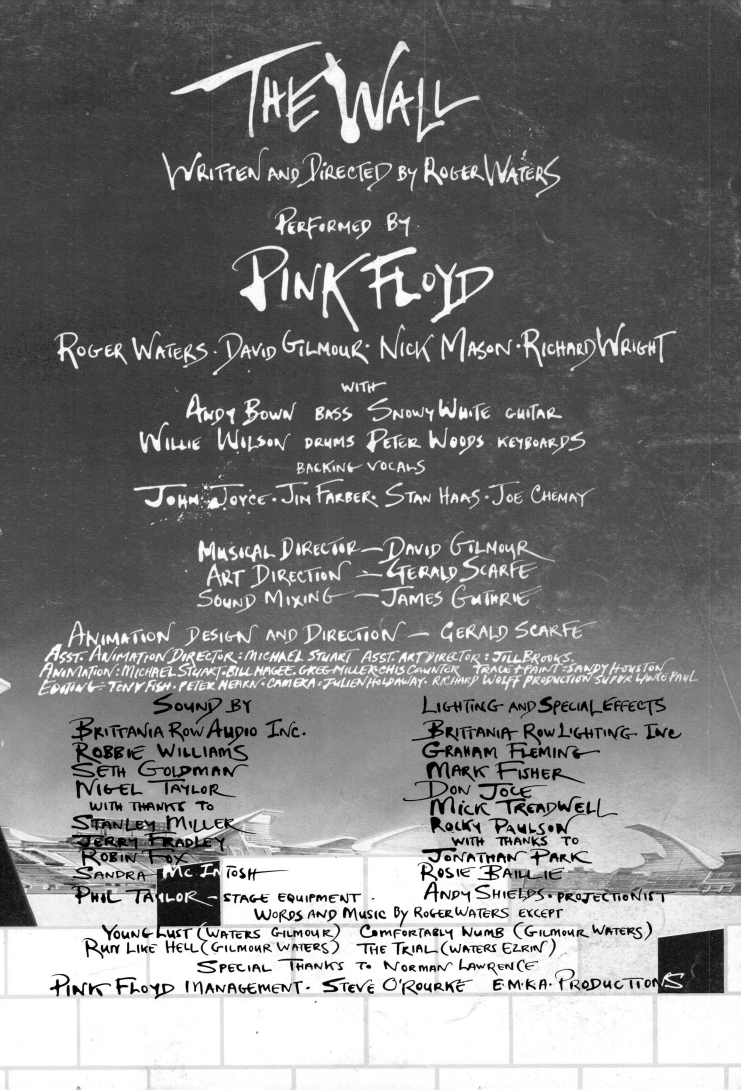

THE WALL

WRITTEN AND DIRECTED BY ROGER WATERS

PERFORMED BY

PINK FLOYD

ROGER WATERS · DAVID GILMOUR · NICK MASON · RICHARD WRIGHT

WITH

ANDY BOWN BASS SNOWY WHITE GUITAR
WILLIE WILSON DRUMS PETER WOODS KEYBOARDS
BACKING VOCALS
JOHN JOYCE · JIM FARBER · STAN HAAS · JOE CHEMAY

MUSICAL DIRECTOR — DAVID GILMOUR
ART DIRECTION — GERALD SCARFE
SOUND MIXING — JAMES GUTHRIE

ANIMATION DESIGN AND DIRECTION — GERALD SCARFE
ASST. ANIMATION DIRECTOR : MICHAEL STUART ASST. ART DIRECTOR : JILL BROOKS.
ANIMATION : MICHAEL STUART · BILL HAGEE · GREG MILLER · CHRIS COUNTER   TRACE & PAINT : SANDY HOUSTON
EDITING : TONY FISH · PETER NEARN · CAMERA : JULIEN HOLDAWAY · RICHARD WOLFF PRODUCTION SUPVR LANCE PAUL

SOUND BY
BRITTANIA ROW AUDIO INC.
ROBBIE WILLIAMS
SETH GOLDMAN
NIGEL TAYLOR
WITH THANKS TO
STANLEY MILLER
JERRY FRADLEY
ROBIN FOX
SANDRA MC INTOSH
PHIL TAYLOR — STAGE EQUIPMENT.

LIGHTING AND SPECIAL EFFECTS
BRITTANIA ROW LIGHTING INC
GRAHAM FLEMING
MARK FISHER
DON JOCE
MICK TREADWELL
ROCKY PAULSON
WITH THANKS TO
JONATHAN PARK
ROSIE BAILLIE
ANDY SHIELDS · PROJECTIONIST

WORDS AND MUSIC BY ROGER WATERS EXCEPT
YOUNG LUST (WATERS GILMOUR) COMFORTABLY NUMB (GILMOUR WATERS)
RUN LIKE HELL (GILMOUR WATERS) THE TRIAL (WATERS EZRIN)
SPECIAL THANKS TO NORMAN LAWRENCE
PINK FLOYD MANAGEMENT · STEVE O'ROURKE E·M·K·A· PRODUCTIONS

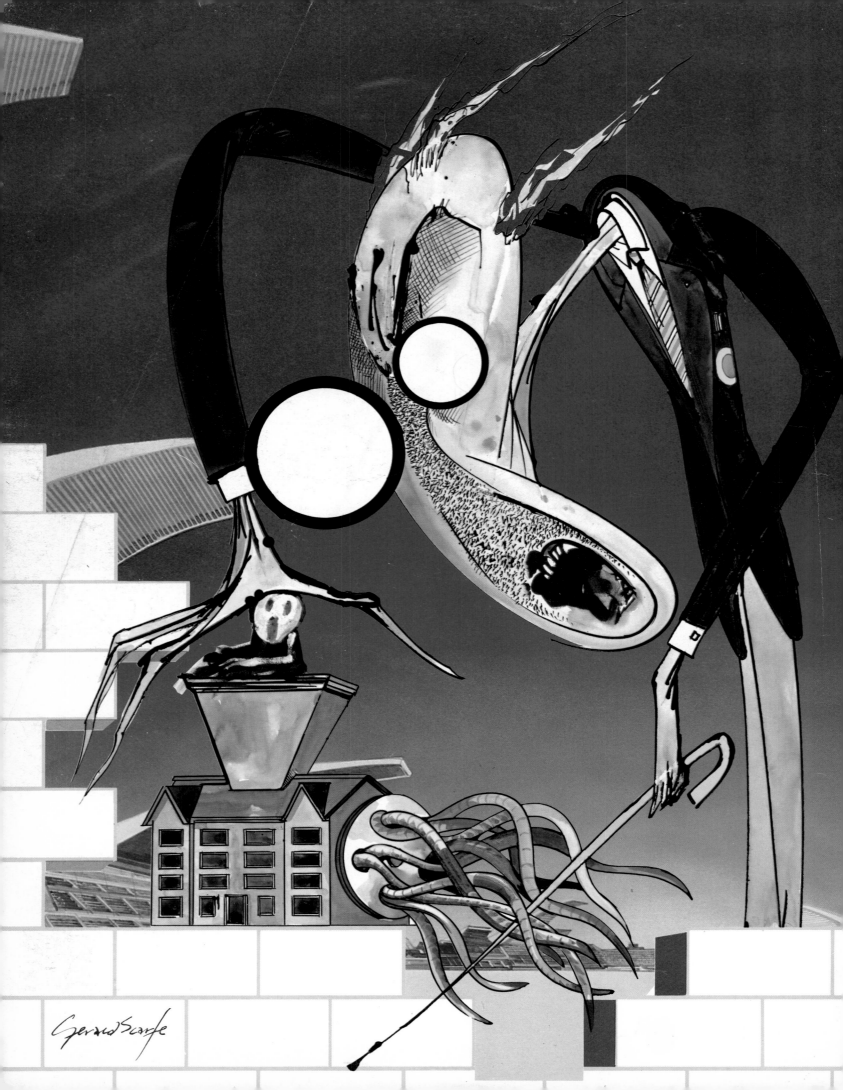

In the Flesh?

So ya
Thought ya
Might like to go to the show
To feel the warm thrill of confusion
That space cadet glow
Tell me is something eluding you sunshine?
Is this not what you expected to see?
If you'd like to find out whats behind these cold eyes?
You'll just have to claw your way through the
Disguise

The Thin Ice

Mamma loves her baby
And daddy loves you too
And the sea may look warm to you babe
And the sky may look blue
But Ooooh babe
Ooooh baby blue
Ooooh babe
If you should go skating
On the thin ice of modern life
Dragging behind you the silent reproach
Of a million tear stained eyes
Don't be surprised, when a crack in the ice
Appears under your feet
You slip out of your depth and out of your mind
With your fear flowing out behind you
As you claw the thin ice

Another Brick in the Wall. part 1.

Daddys flown across the ocean
Leaving just a memory
A snap shot in the family album
Daddy what els did you leave for me
Daddy what d'ya leave behind for me
All in all it was just a brick in the wall
All in all it was all just bricks in the wall.

The Happiest Days of our Lives

When we grew up and went to school
There were certain teachers who would
Hurt the children anyway they could
By pouring their derision
Upon anything we did
And exposing every weakness
However carefully hidden by the kids
But in the town it was well known
When they got home at night, their fat and
Psychopathic wives would thrash them
Within inches of their lives

Another Brick in the Wall part 2

We don't need no education
We don't need no thought control
No dark sarcasm in the classroom
Teachers leave the kids alone,
Hey teacher leave us kids alone
All in all its just another brick in the wall
All in all you're just another brick in the wall

Mother

Mother do you think they'll drop the bomb
Mother do you think they'll like the song
Mother do you think they'll try to break my balls
Mother should I build a wall
Mother should I run for president
Mother should I trust the government
Mother will they put me in the firing line
Mother am I really dying.
Hush now baby don't you cry
Mama's gonna make all of your
Nightmares come true
Mama's gonna put all of her fears into you
Mama's gonna keep you right here
Under her wing
She won't let you fly but she might let you sing
Mama will keep baby cosy and warm
Ooooh Babe Ooooh Babe Ooooh Babe
Of course Mama'll help build the wall

Mother do you think she's good enough for me
Mother do you think she's dangerous to me
Mother will she tear your little boy apart
Mother will she break my heart.

Hush now baby, baby don't you cry
Mama's gonna check out all your girlfriends for you
Mama won't let anyone dirty get through
Mama's gonna wait up till you come in
Mama will always find out where
You've been
Mama's gonna keep you healthy and clean
Ooooh Babe Ooooh Babe Ooooh Babe
You'll always be a baby to me
Mother, did it need to be so high.

Gerald Scarfe

Goodbye Blue Sky

Ooooooooooooooooh
Did you see the frightened ones
Did you hear the falling bombs
Did you ever wonder
Why we had to run for shelter
When the promise of a brave new world
Unfurled beneath a clear blue sky
Ooooooooooooooooh
Did you see the frightened ones
Did you hear the falling bombs
The flames are all long gone
But the pain lingers on
Goodbye Blue Sky
Goodbye Blue Sky
Goodbye

Empty Spaces / What shall we do now.?

What shall we use to fill the empty
Spaces where we used to talk
How shall I fill the final places
How shall I complete the wall

Shall we buy a new guitar
Shall we drive a more powerful car
Shall we work straight through the night
Shall we get into fights
Leave the lights on
Drop bombs
Do tours of the east
Contract diseases
Bury bones
Break up homes
Send flowers by phone
Take to drink
Go to shrinks
Give up meat
Rarely sleep
Keep people as pets
Train dogs
Race rats
Fill the attic with cash
Bury treasure
Store up leisure
But never relax at all
With our backs to the wall

Don't Leave me now

Oooh Babe
Don't leave me now.
Don't say its the end of the road
Remember the flowers I sent
I need you Babe
To put through the shredder
In front of my friends
Ooooh Babe
Don't leave me now?
How could you go?
When you know how I need you.
To beat to a pulp on a Saturday night
Ooooh Babe
Don't leave me now
How can you treat me this way
Running away
I need you Babe
Why are you running away?
Ooooooh Babe!

Another Brick in the Wall
part 3

I don't need no arms around me
I don't need no drugs to calm me
I have seen the writing on the wall
Don't think I'll need anything at all
No don't think I'll need anything at all
All in All it was all just bricks in the wall
All in All you were all just bricks in the wall

Goodbye Cruel World

Goodbye cruel world
I'm leaving you today
Goodbye
Goodbye
Goodbye
Goodbye all you people
There's nothing you can say
to make me change
My mind
Goodbye.

Young Lust

I am just a new boy
A stranger in this town
Where are all the good times
Who's gonna show this stranger around?
Who? Who? Who? Who?
Ooooooooh I need a dirty woman
Ooooooooh I need a dirty girl
Will some cold woman in this desert land
Make me feel like a real man
Take this rock and roll refugee
Oooh Babe set me free
Oooh, Oooh, Oooh, Ooh
Ooooooooh I need a dirty woman
Ooooooooh I need a dirty girl.

One of my turns

Day after day, love turns grey
Like the skin of a dying man
Night after night, we pretend it's all right
But I have grown older and
You have grown colder and
Nothing is very much fun any more.

And I can feel one of my turns coming on.
I feel cold as a razor blade
Tight as a tourniquet
Dry as a funeral drum,
Run to the bedroom, in the suitcase on the left
You'll find my favourite axe
Don't look so frightened
This is just a passing phase
Just one of my bad days
Would you like to watch T.V.?
Or get between the sheets?
Or contemplate the silent freeway?
Would you like something to eat?
Would you like to learn to fly?
Would you like to see me try?
Would you like to call the cops?
Do you think it's time I stopped?
Why are you running away?

Hey you

Hey you! out there in the cold
Getting lonely, getting old, can you feel me
Hey you! standing in the aisles
With itchy feet and fading smiles, can you feel me
Hey you! don't help them to bury the light
Don't give in without a fight.

Hey you! out there on your own
Sitting naked by the phone would you touch me
Hey you! with your ear against the wall
Waiting for someone to call out would you touch me
Hey you! would you help me to carry the stone
Open your heart, I'm coming home

But it was only fantasy
The wall was too high, as you can see
No matter how he tried he could not break free
And the worms ate into his brain.

Hey you! out there on the road
Doing what you're told, can you help me
Hey you! out there beyond the wall
Breaking bottles in the hall, can you help me
Hey you! don't tell me there's no hope at all
Together we stand, divided we fall.

Is there anybody out there?

Is there anybody out there?

Nobody Home

I've got a little black book with my poems in
I've got a bag with a toothbrush and a comb in
When I'm a good dog they sometimes throw me a bone in
I got elastic bands keeping my shoes on
Got those swollen hand blues
Got thirteen channels of shit on the T.V. to choose from
I've got electric light
And I've got second sight
I've got amazing powers of observation
And that is how I know
When I try to get through
On the telephone to you
There'll be nobody home
I've got the obligatory Hendrix perm
And the inevitable pinhole burns
All down the front of my favourite satin shirt
I've got nicotine stains on my fingers
I've got a silver spoon on a chain
I've got a grand piano to prop up my mortal remains
I've got wild staring eyes
I've got a strong urge to fly
But I've got nowhere to fly to
Ooooh Babe when I pick up the phone
There's still nobody home
I've got a pair of Gohills boots
And I've got fading roots.

Vera

Does anybody here remember Vera Lynn
Remember how she said that
We would meet again
Some sunny day
Vera! Vera!
What has become of you
Does anybody else in here
Feel the way I do.

Bring the boys back home

Bring the boys back home
Bring the boys back home
Don't leave the children on their own
Bring the boys back home

Comfortably Numb -

Hello,
Is there anybody in there
Just nod if you can hear me
Is there anyone at home
Come on now,
I hear you're feeling down
I can ease your pain
And get you on your feet again
Relax
I'll need some information first
Just the basic facts
Can you show me where it hurts

There is no pain, you are receding
A distant ship, smoke on the horizon
You are only coming through in waves
Your lips move but I can't hear what you're saying
When I was a child I had a fever
My hands felt just like two balloons
Now I've got that feeling once again
I can't explain, you would not understand
This is not how I am
I have become comfortably numb -

O.K.
Just a little pin prick
There'll be no more aaaaaaaah !
But you may feel a little sick
Can you stand up ?
I do believe it's working, good
That'll keep you going through the show
Come on it's time to go.
There is no pain, you are receding
A distant ship, smoke on the horizon
You are only coming through in waves
Your lips move but I can't hear what you're saying
When I was a child
I caught a fleeting glimpse
Out of the corner of my eye
I turned to look but it was gone
I cannot put my finger on it now
The child is grown
The dream is gone
And I have become
Comfortably numb -

The Show must go on.

Oooh Ma Oooh Pa
Does the show have to go on
Oooh Pa take me home
Oooh Ma let me go
Do I have to stand up
Wild eyed in the spotlight
What a nightmare why !
Don't I turn and run
There must be some mistake
I didn't mean to let them
Take away my soul
Am I too old is it too late
Oooh Ma Oooh Pa
Where has the feeling gone ?
Oooh Ma Oooh Pa
Will I remember the songs ?
The show must go on.

Gerald Scarfe

Waiting for the Worms.

Ooooh You cannot reach me now
Ooooh No matter how you try
Goodbye cruel world it's over
Walk on by
Sitting in a bunker here behind my wall
Waiting for the worms to come
In perfect isolation here behind my wall
Waiting for the worms to come
Waiting to cut out the deadwood
Waiting to clean up the city
Waiting to follow the worms
Waiting to put on a blackshirt
Waiting to weed out the weaklings
Waiting to smash in their windows
And kick in their doors.

Waiting for the final solution
To strengthen the strain
Waiting to follow the worms
Waiting to turn on the showers
And fire the ovens
Waiting for the queens and the coons
and the reds and the Jews
Waiting to follow the worms
Would you like to see Britannia
Rule again my friend
All you have to do is follow the worms
Would you like to send our coloured cousins
Home again my friend
All you need to do is follow the worms.

For the Flesh

So ya
Thought ya
Might like to
Go to the show
To feel the warm thrill of confusion
That space cadet glow
I've got some bad news for you sunshine
Pink isn't well he stayed back at the hotel
And they sent us along as a surrogate band
And we're going to find out where you fans
Really stand
Are there any queers in the theatre tonight
Get 'em up against the wall
There's one in the spotlight
He don't look right to me
Get him up against the wall
That one looks Jewish
And that one's a coon
Who let all this riff raff into the room
There's one smoking a joint and
Another with spots
If I had my way
I'd have all of you shot

Stop

Stop
I wanna go home
Take off this uniform
And leave the show
And I'm waiting in this cell
Because I have to know
Have I been guilty all this time

Run like Hell.

You better run like hell
You better make your face up in
Your favourite disguise
With your button down lips and your
Roller blind eyes
With your empty smile
And your hungry heart
Feel the bile rising from your guilty past
With your nerves in tatters
When the cockleshell shatters
And the hammers batter
Down the door
You better run like hell

You better run all day
And run all night
And keep your dirty feelings
Deep inside. And if you
Take your girlfriend
Out tonight,
You better park the car
Well out of sight
Cos if they catch you in the back seat
Trying to pick her locks
They're gonna send you back to mother
In a cardboard box
You better run.

Outside the Wall

All alone, or in twos
The ones who really love you
Walk up and down outside the wall
Some hand in hand
Some gathering together in bands
The bleeding hearts and artists
Make their stand
And when they've given you their all
Some stagger and falls after all its not easy
Banging your heart against some mad buggers
Wall

PINK FLOYD THE WALL

Legend of Musical Symbols

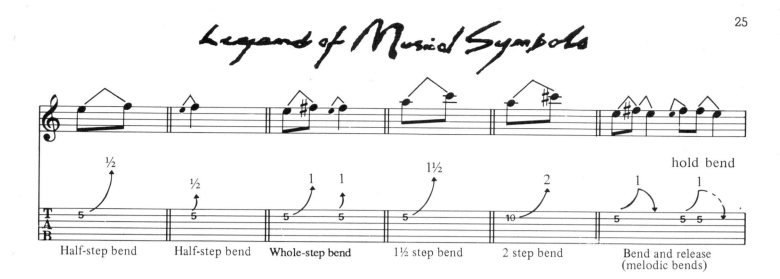

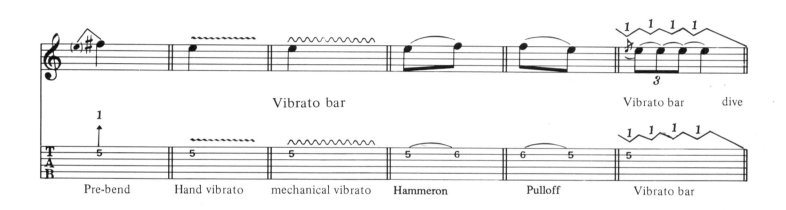

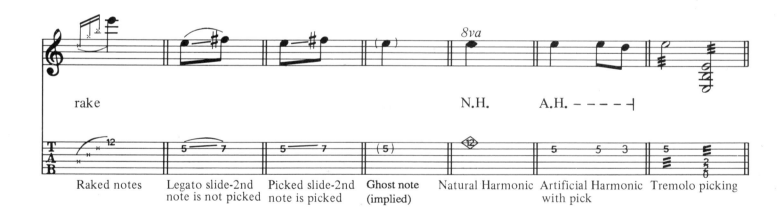

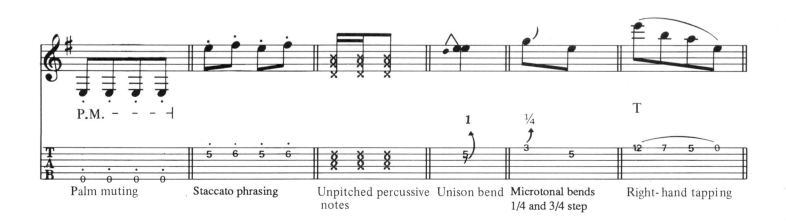

In the Flesh?

Moderately slow ♩ = 151

Intro

electric guitar 1 with distortion

Words & Music by
ROGER WATERS

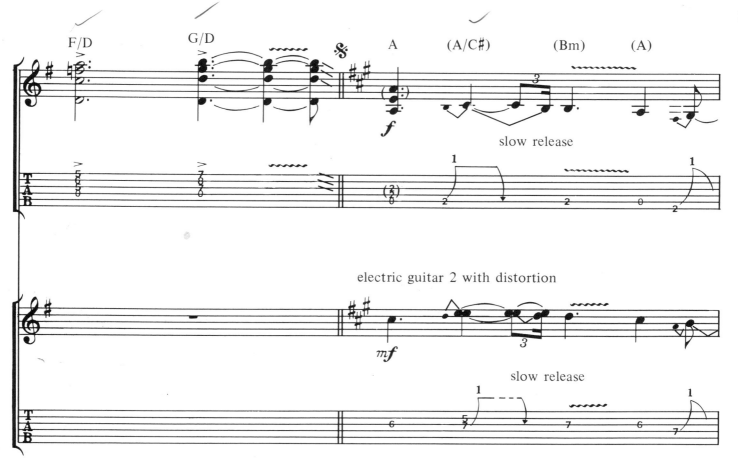

electric guitar 2 with distortion

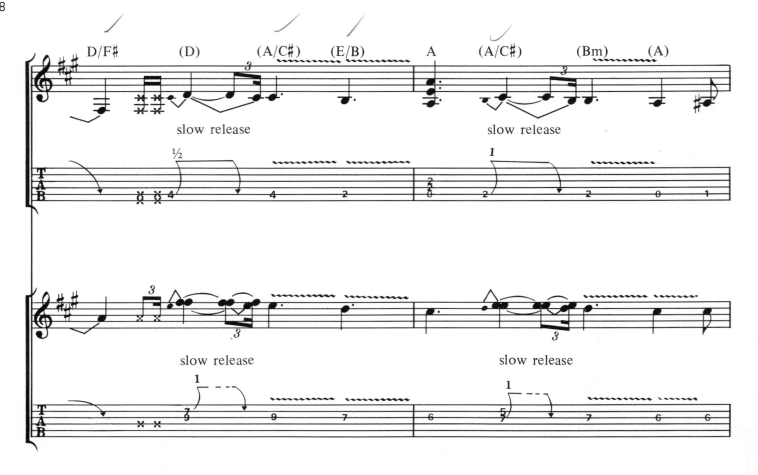

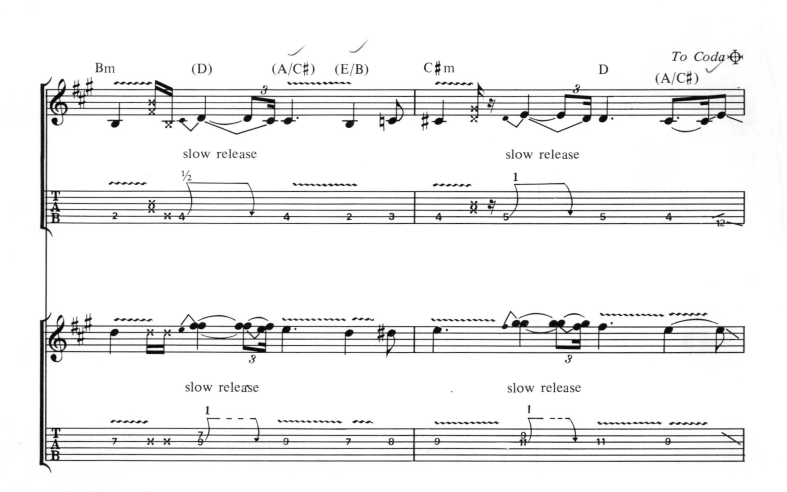

The Thin Ice

Words & Music by
ROGER WATERS

Slowly ♩ = 110

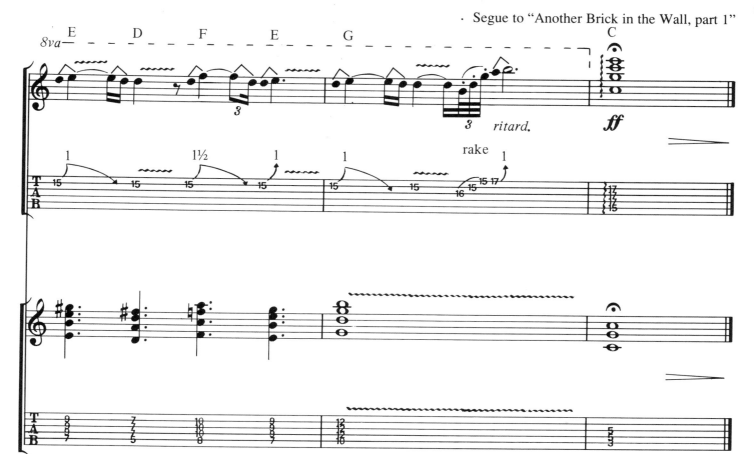

Another Brick in the Wall, part 1.

Moderately ♩ = 100

Words & Music by
ROGER WATERS

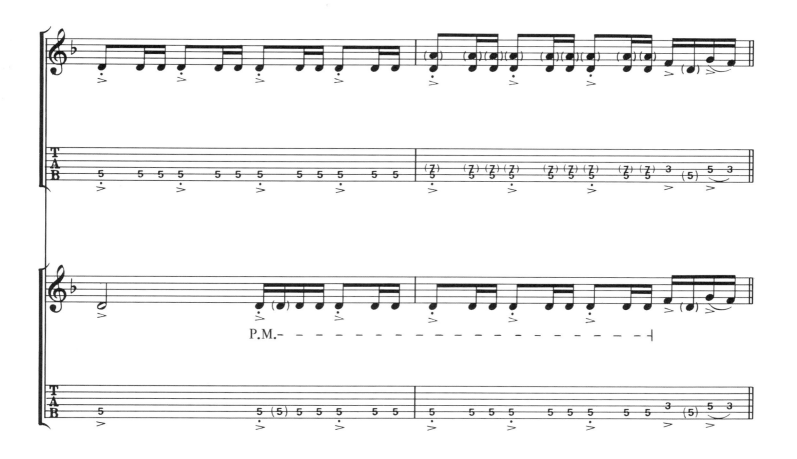

Verse 1

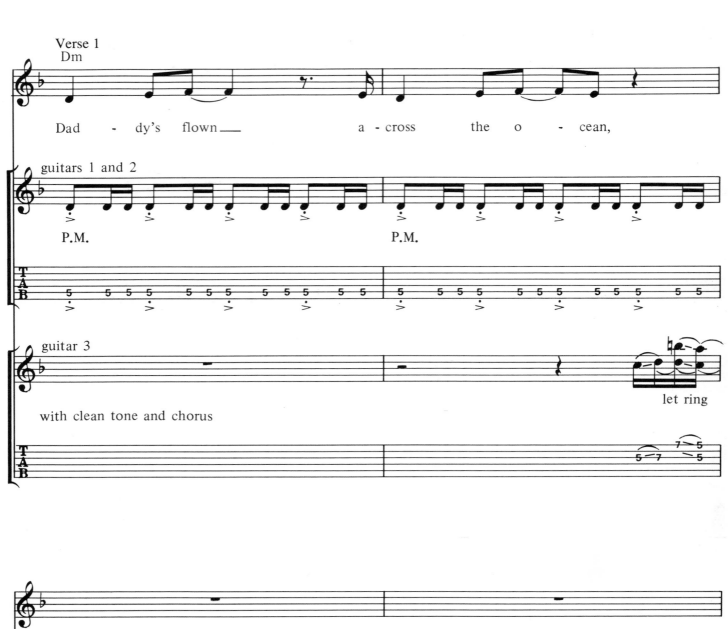

Dad - dy's flown ____ a - cross the o - cean,

leav - ing just ____ a mem - o - ry. ____

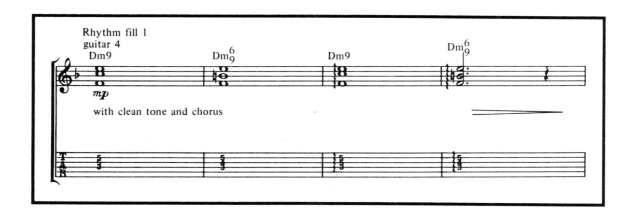

The snap - shot in the

fam - 'ly al - bum.

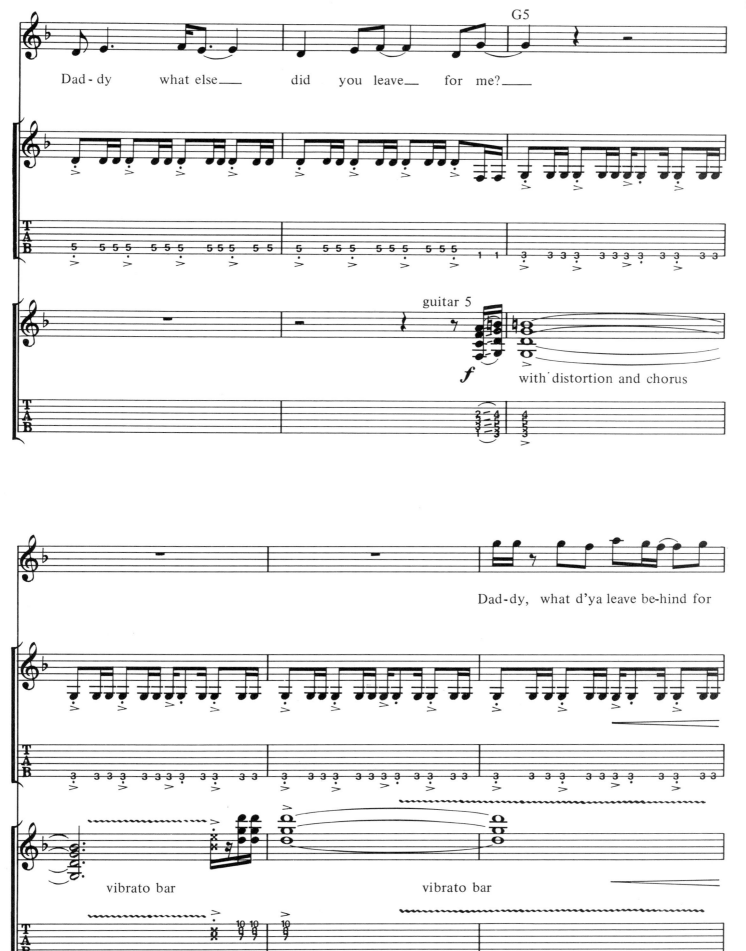

me?

All in all— it was—

just a brick in— the wall.

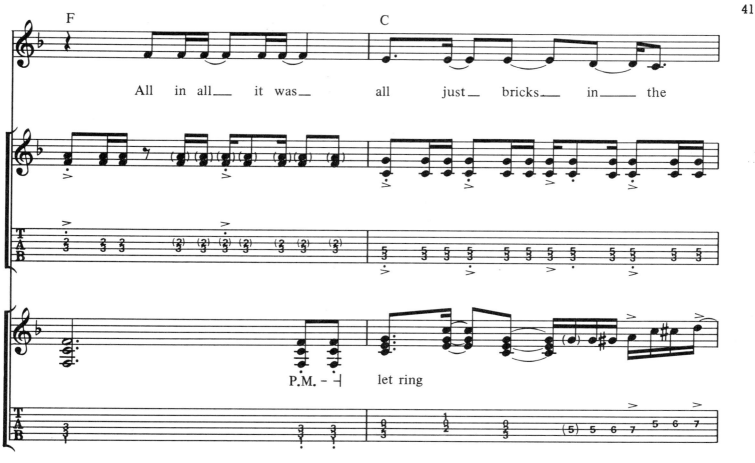

All in all___ it was___ all just___ bricks___ in___ the

wall.

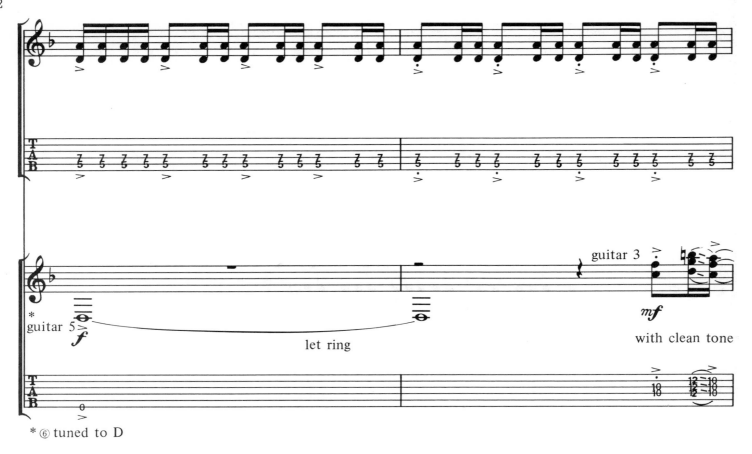

*guitar 5
let ring
guitar 3
with clean tone

* ⑥ tuned to D

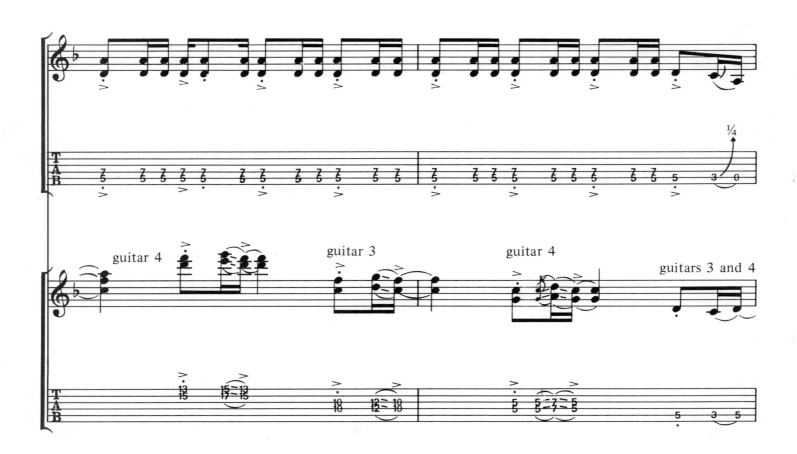

guitar 4
guitar 3
guitar 4
guitars 3 and 4

44

guitar 4

guitars 3 and 4

let ring

with schoolyard sound effects

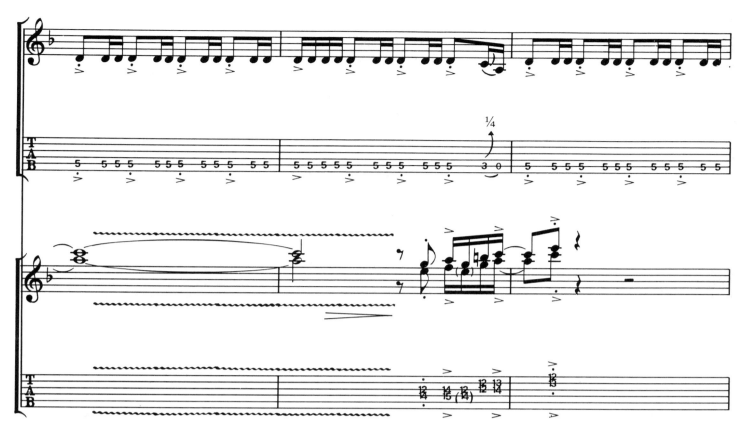

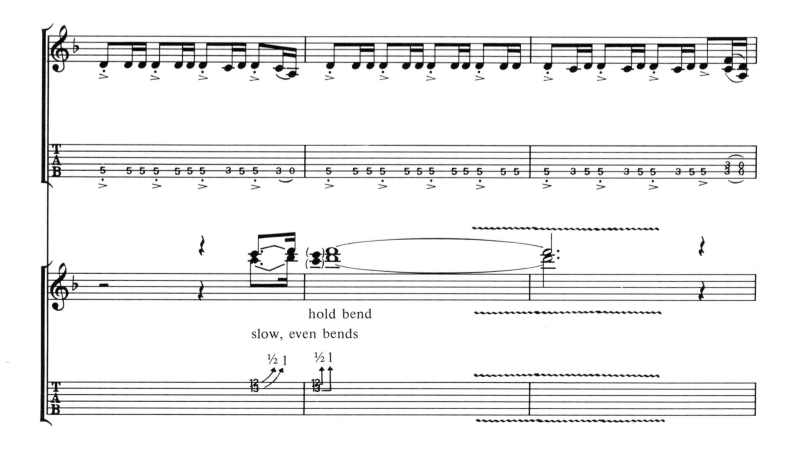

hold bend

slow, even bends

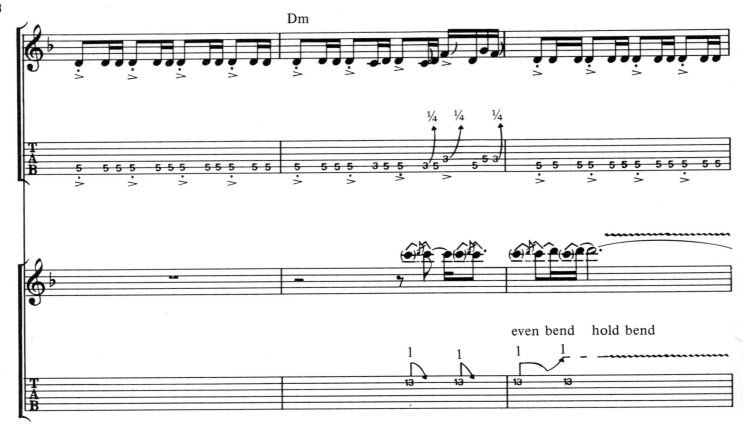

fade in helicopter sound effects

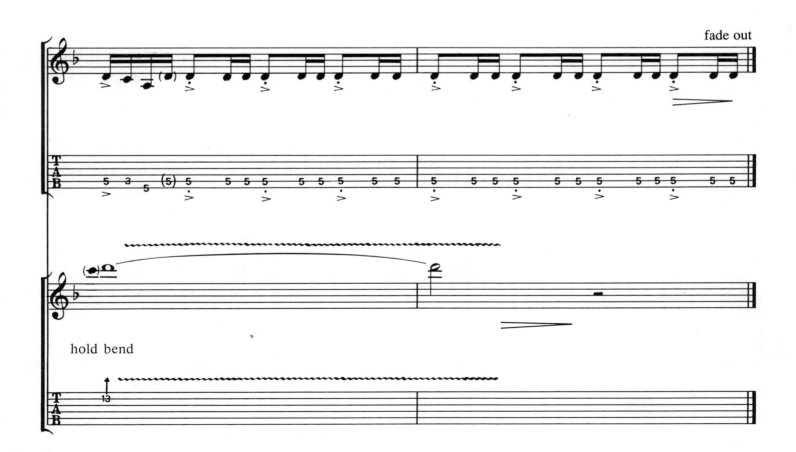

fade out

hold bend

The Happiest Days of our Lives

Words & Music by
ROGER WATERS

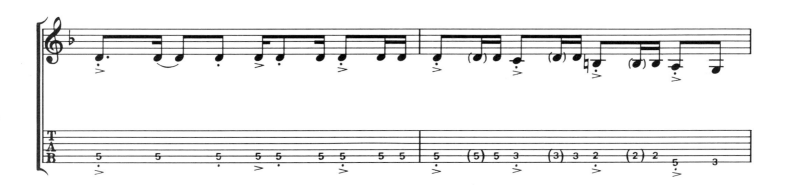

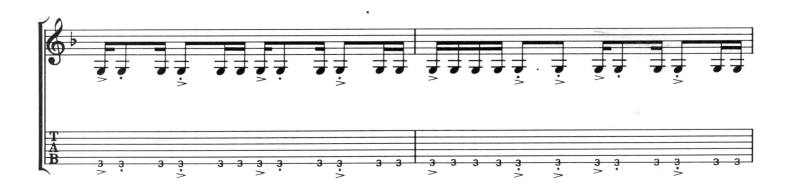

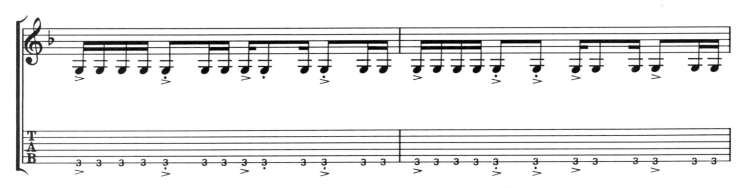

52

By pour - ing their de - ri - sion _____ up - on

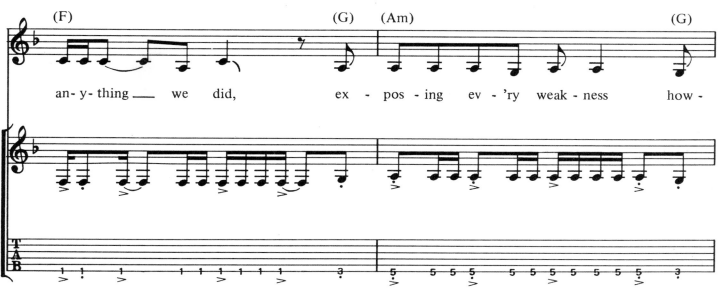

an - y - thing ___ we did, ex - pos - ing ev - 'ry weak - ness how -

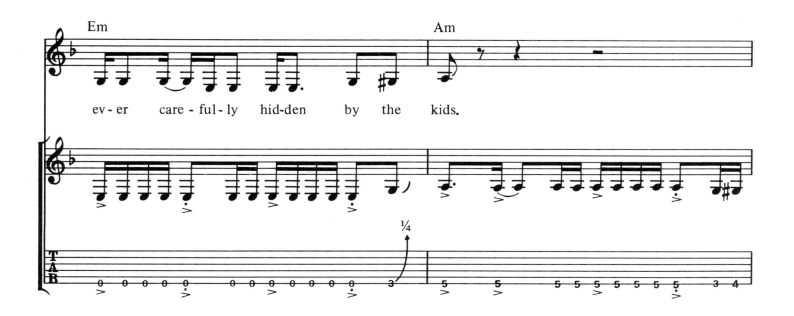

ev - er care - ful - ly hid - den by the kids.

But in___ the town it was___ well known when they got

home at night, their fat and psy-cho-path-ic wives___would thrash them___ with in

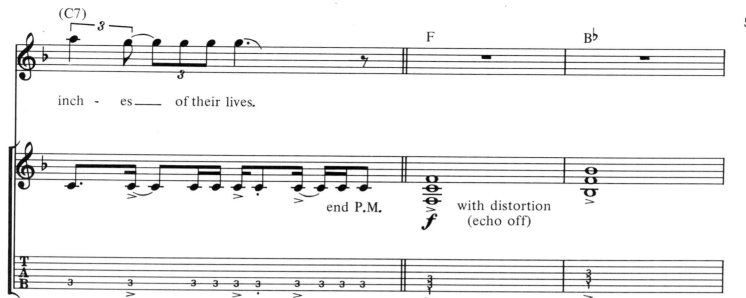

inch - es ___ of their lives.

Segue directly to "Another Brick in the Wall, part 2"

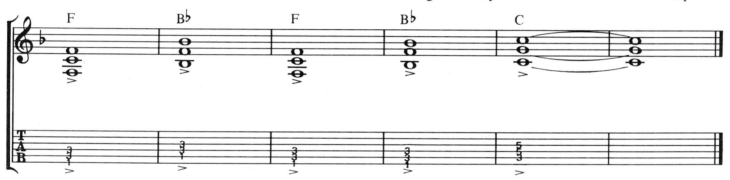

Another Brick in the Wall, part 2.

Words & Music by
ROGER WATERS

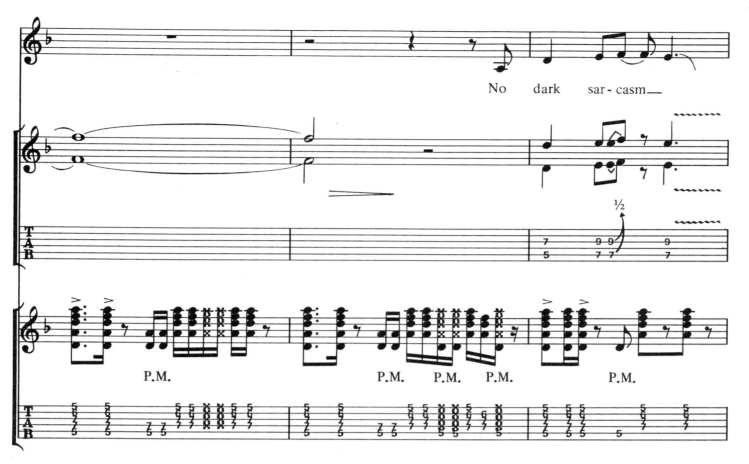

No dark sar-casm—

in the class-room.

Teach - er leave_them kids a - lone.—

P.M.

with Fill 1

½

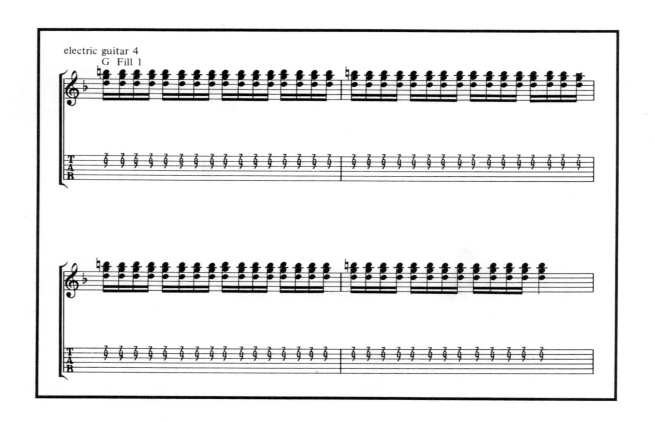

electric guitar 4
G Fill 1

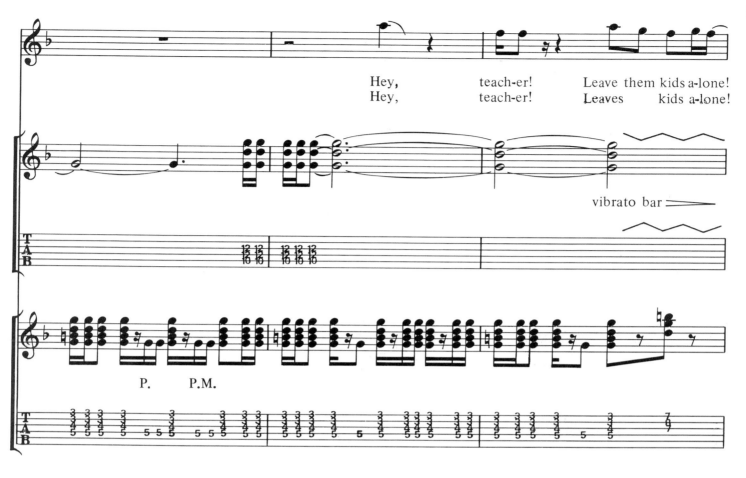

Hey,   teach-er!   Leave them kids a-lone!
Hey,   teach-er!   Leaves   kids a-lone!

vibrato bar

P.   P.M.

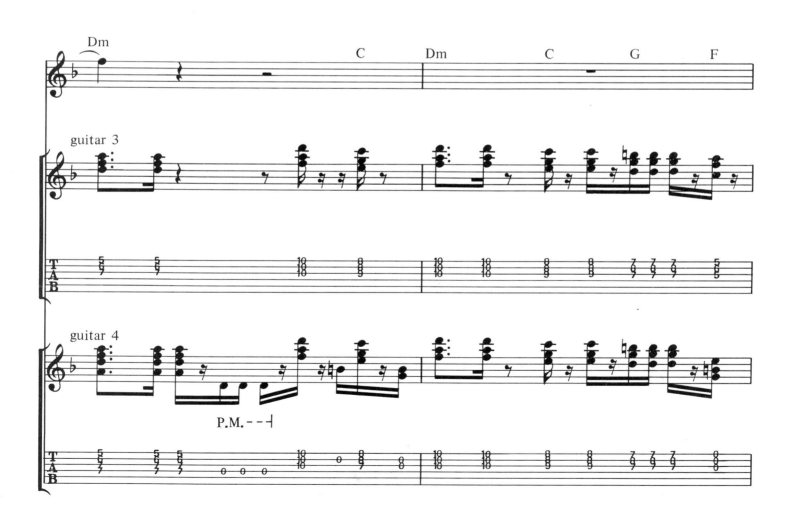

Dm   C   Dm   C   G   F

guitar 3

guitar 4

P.M.

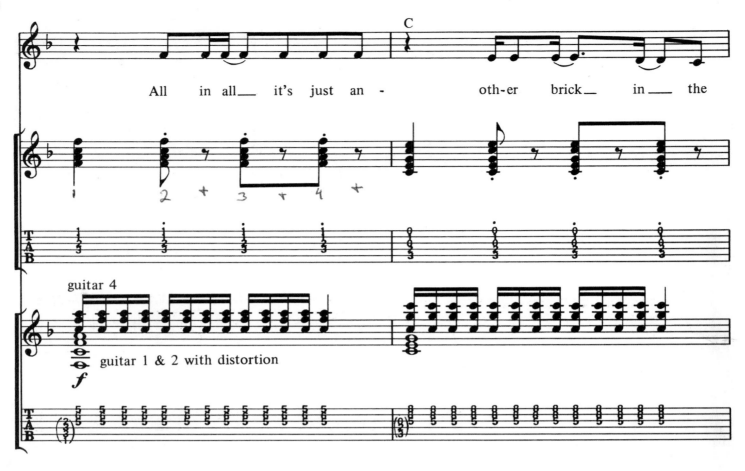

All   in all___ it's just an - oth-er brick___ in ___ the

guitar 4

guitar 1 & 2 with distortion

wall.

let ring   P.M.   let ring   P.M.

let ring   P.M.

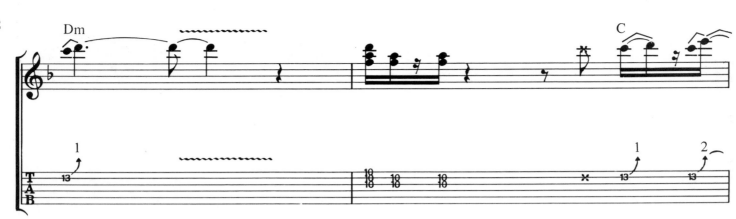

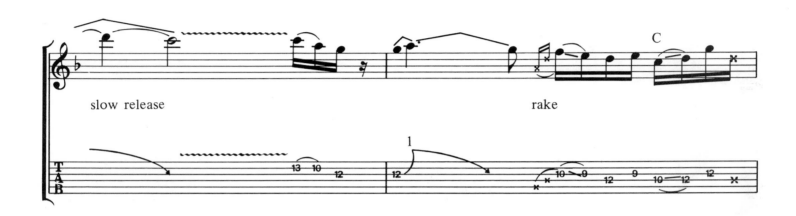

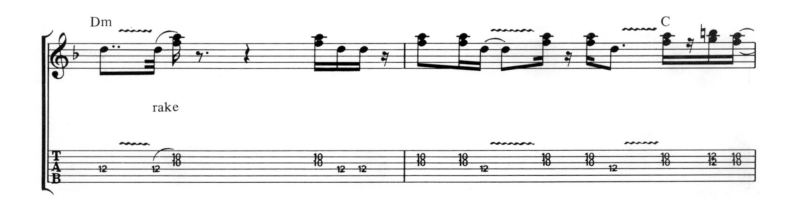

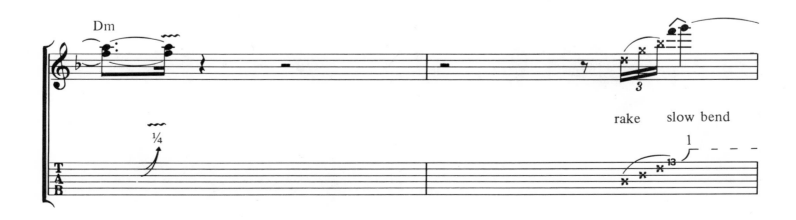

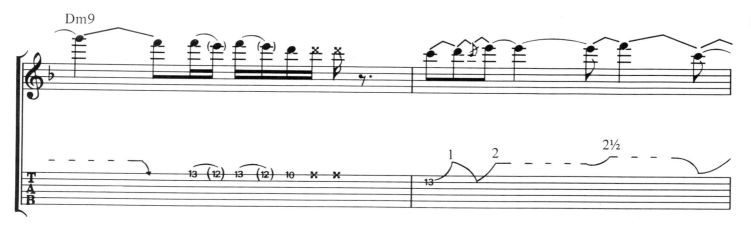

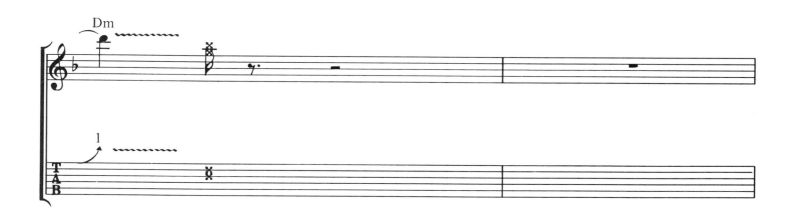

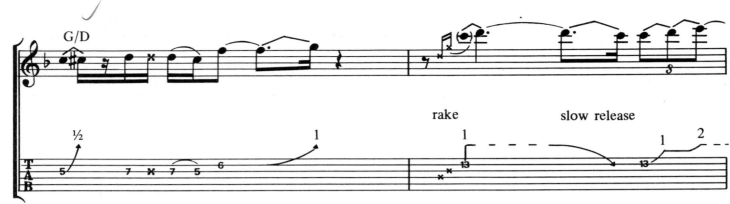

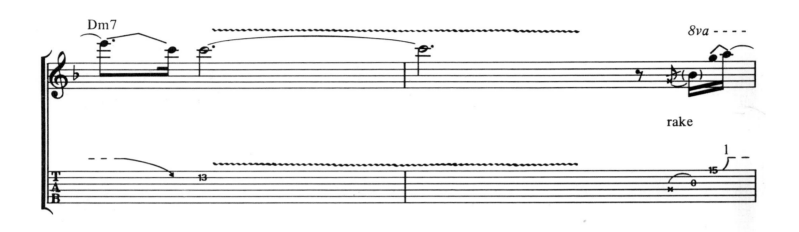

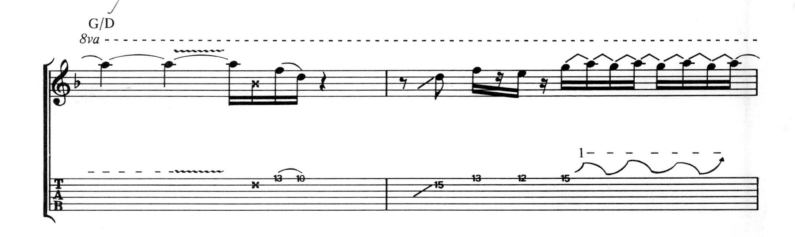

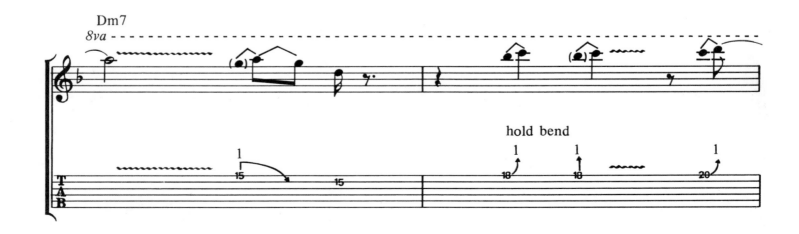

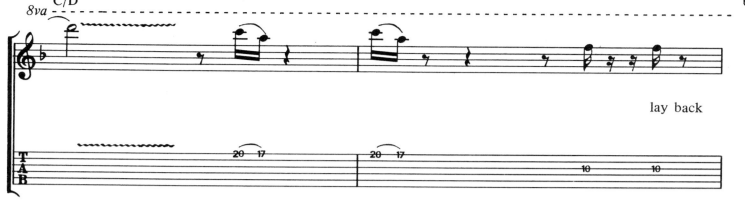

lay back

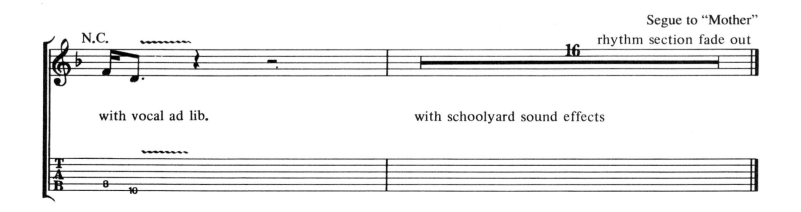

Segue to "Mother"
rhythm section fade out

with vocal ad lib.

with schoolyard sound effects

Mother

Moderately with half-time feel ♪= 134

Words & Music by
ROGER WATERS

schoolyard and phone effects for
approximately 16 seconds   (Sigh!) Moth - er, do you think they'll drop___ the

acoustic guitar 1

Rhythm figure 1

Bomb?

let ring

let ring

Moth- er, do you think they'll like___ this song?

let ring

D(sus4)   G

Moth-er, do you think they'll try___ to _____ break my

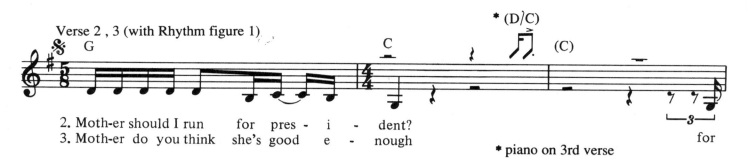

Verse 2 , 3 (with Rhythm figure 1)

* (D/C) (C)

2. Moth-er should I run   for   pres - i - dent?
3. Moth-er do you think   she's good   e - nough

* piano on 3rd verse

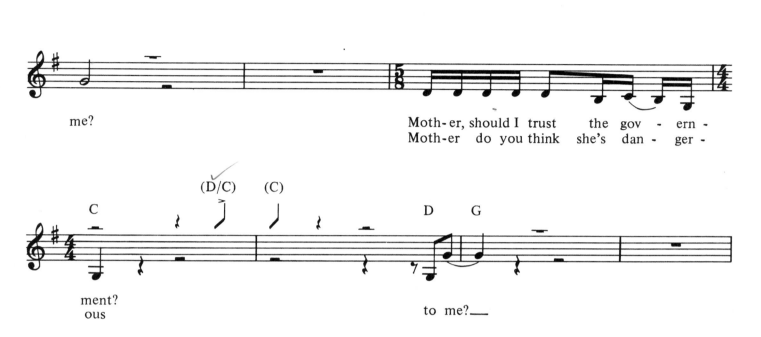

me?

Moth-er, should I trust   the   gov - ern -
Moth-er do you think   she's   dan - ger -

(D/C)   (C)   D   G

ment?
ous   to me?___

Moth-er, will they put   me in ___ the   fir - ing   line?
Moth-er, will she tear   your lit-tle boy_____ a - part?

(Dsus2)   D

Ooh,
Ooh,

12 string acoustic guitar

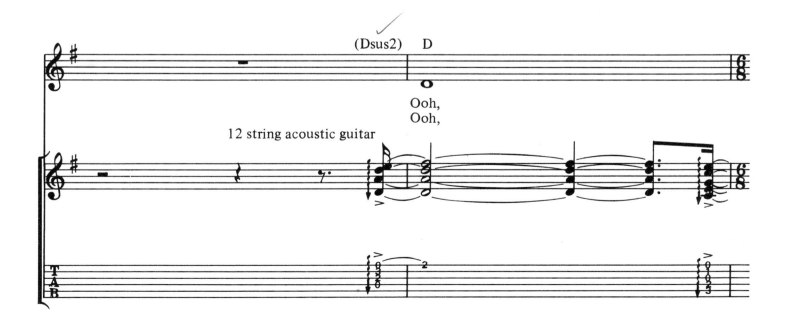

Ah,   is it just a waste   of   time?_____
Ah,   moth- er will she break   my   heart?_____

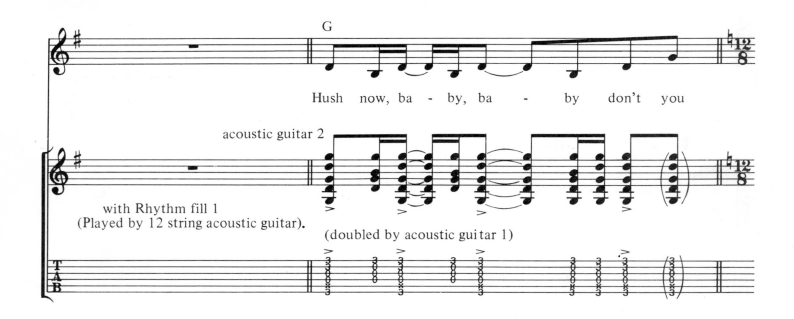

Hush now, ba - by, ba -   by   don't   you

acoustic guitar 2

with Rhythm fill 1
(Played by 12 string acoustic guitar).

(doubled by acoustic guitar 1)

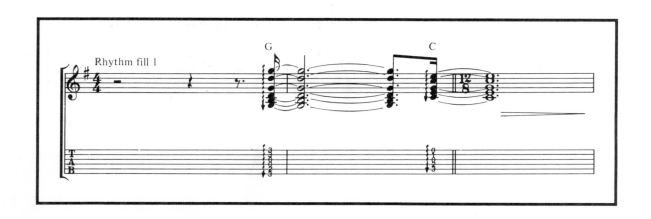

Rhythm fill 1

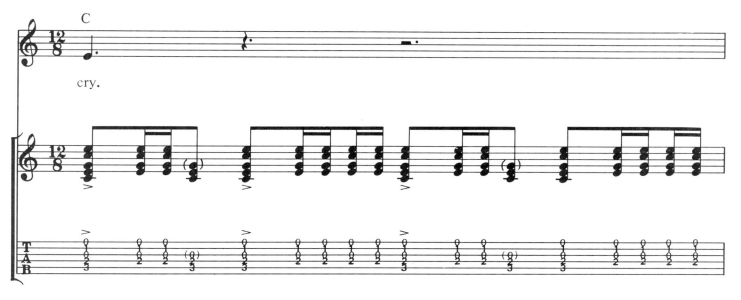

cry.

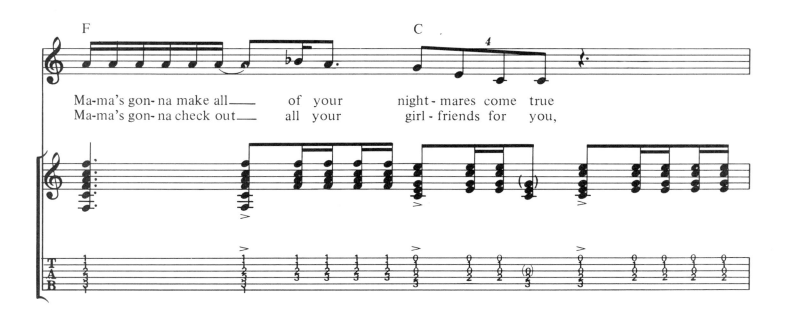

Ma-ma's gon- na make all___ of your night- mares come true
Ma-ma's gon- na check out___ all your girl - friends for you,

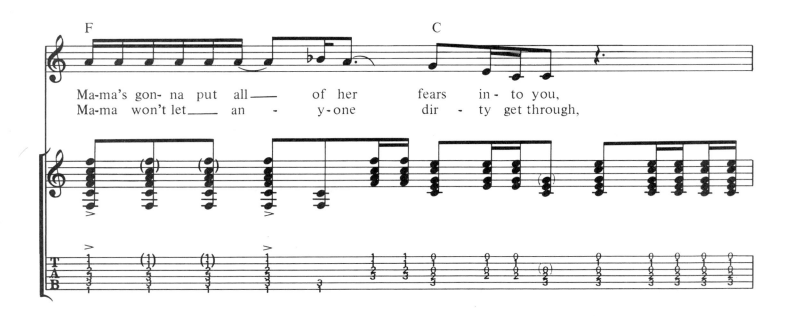

Ma-ma's gon- na put all___ of her fears in - to you,
Ma-ma won't let___ an - y-one dir - ty get through,

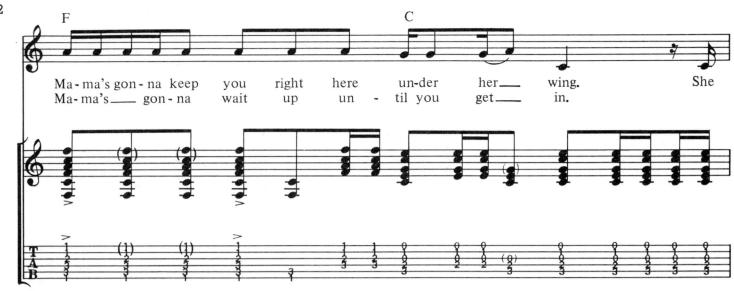

Ma-ma's gon-na keep you right here un-der her___ wing. She
Ma-ma's___ gon-na wait up un - til you get___ in.

won't let you fly_____ but she might let you sing,
Ma - ma will al - ways find out where you've been,

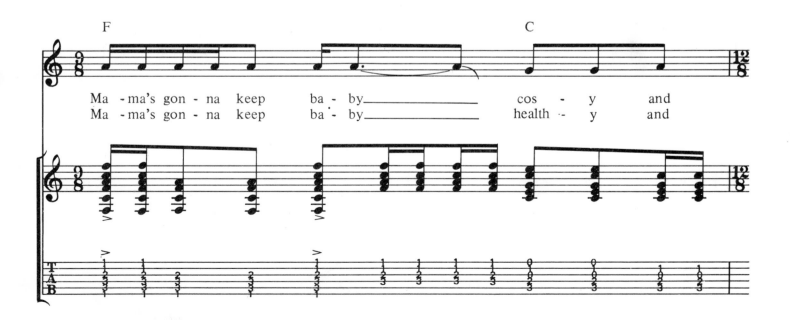

Ma-ma's gon-na keep ba-by_____ cos - y and
Ma-ma's gon-na keep ba-by_____ health - y and

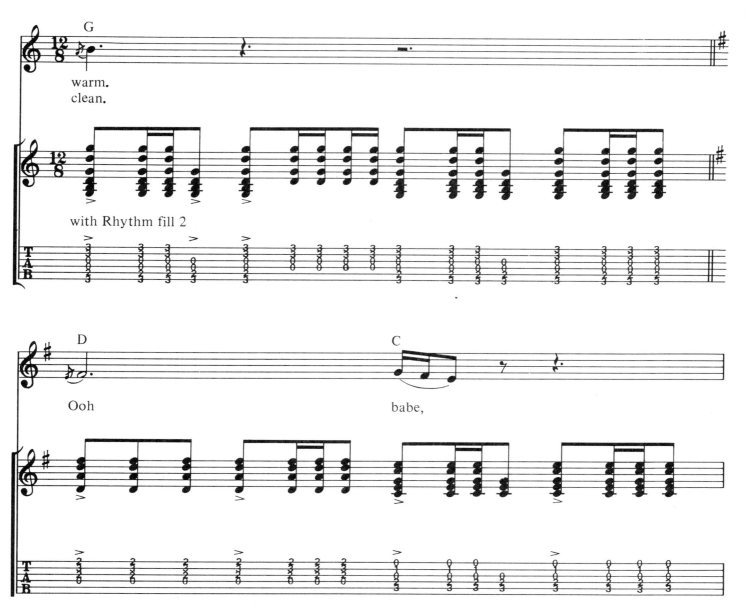

warm.
clean.

with Rhythm fill 2

Ooh babe,

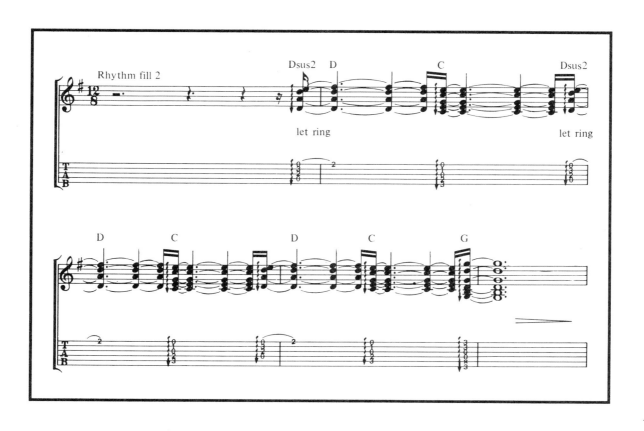

Rhythm fill 2

let ring   let ring

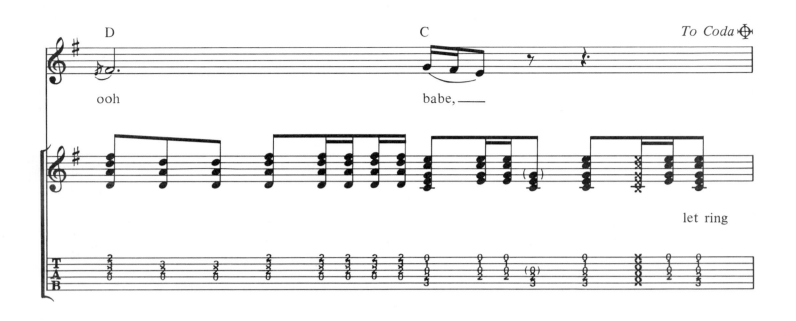

ooh   babe, ——

To Coda ⊕

let ring

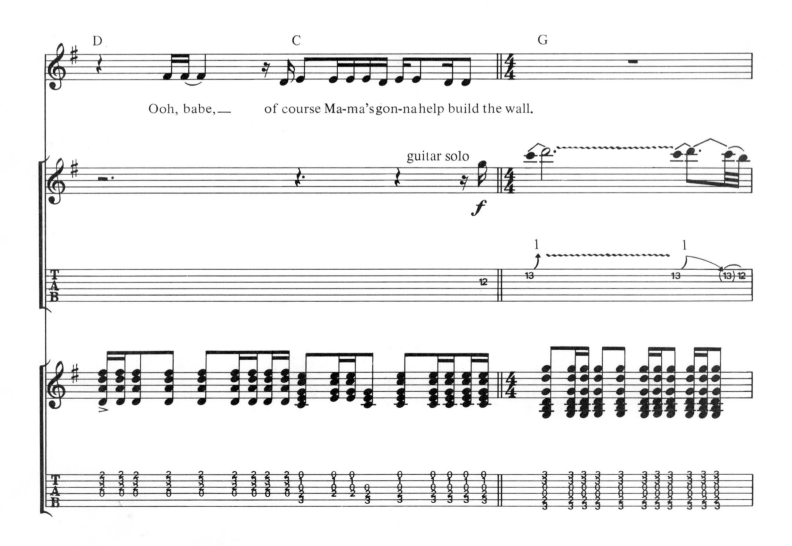

Ooh, babe, ——   of course Ma-ma's gon-na help build the wall.

guitar solo

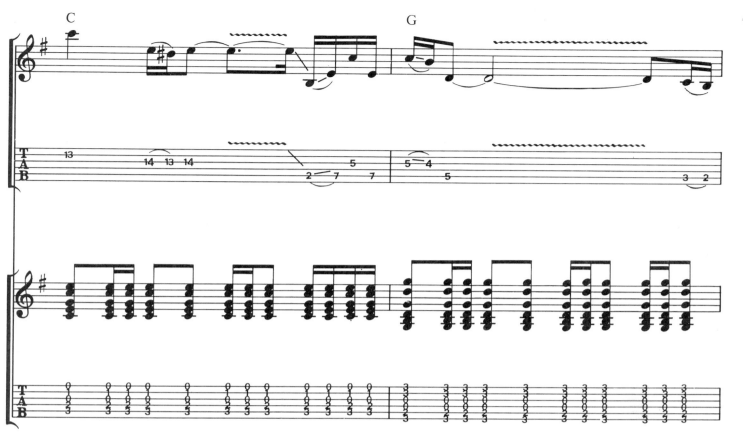

steady gliss.

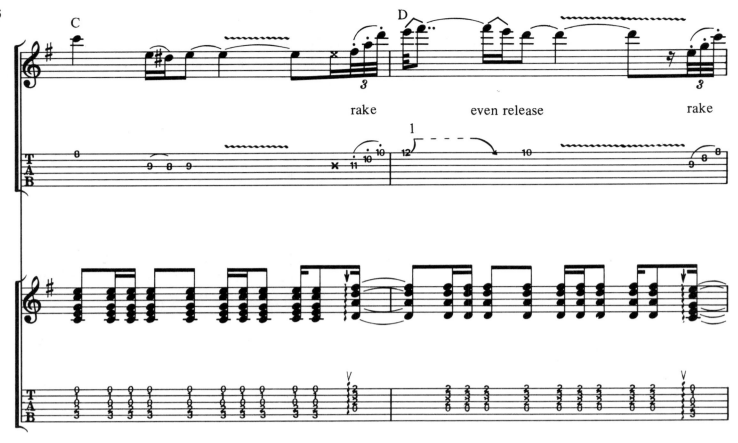

rake   even release   rake

D.S. % al Coda ⊕

Ooh, babe, you'll al - ways be ba - by to

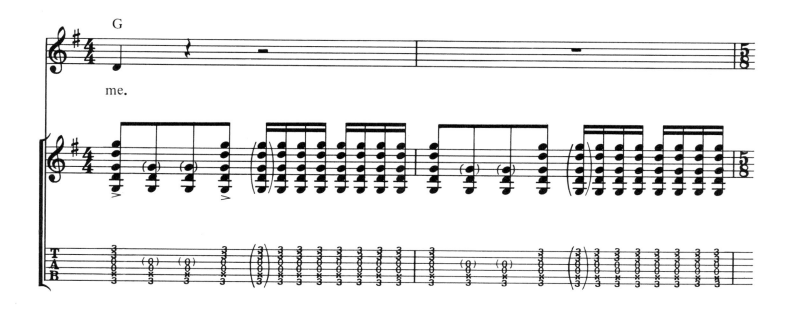

me.

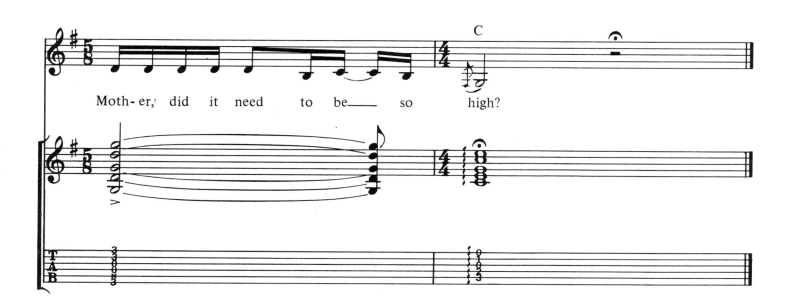

Moth- er, did it need to be___ so high?

Goodbye Blue Sky

Words & Music by
ROGER WATERS

80

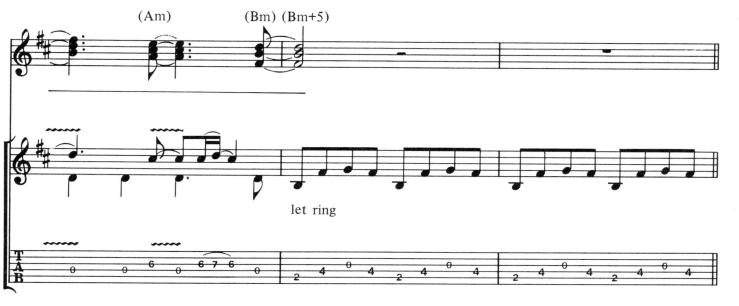

let ring

N.C. (Am)   (B/A)   (Am)

Did, did, did, did you see the fright-ened ones?   Did, did, did, did you hear the

(B/A)   To Coda ⊕ (Am)   (B/A)   (Am)

fall - ing bombs?   Did, did, did, did you ev - er won-der why we had to run for

— but the pain — lin - gers on. —

Chorus

Good - bye, blue — sky, —

Guitar 1 repeats previous measure

Good - bye, — blue - sky, — good - bye, —

good - bye.____

Segue to "Empty Spaces"

fade out

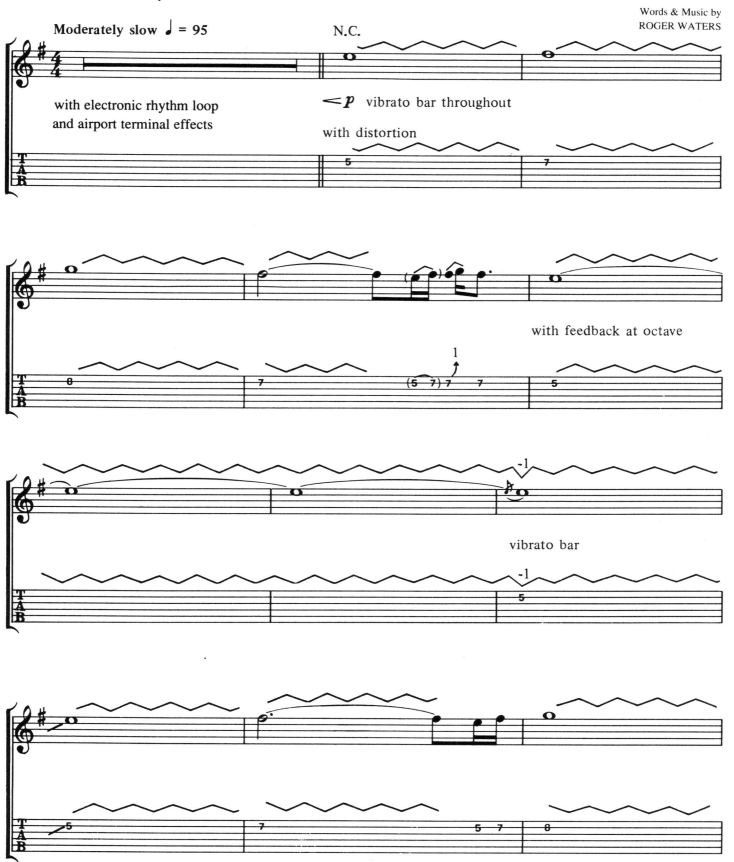

Empty Spaces/What shall we do now?

Words & Music by
ROGER WATERS

with feedback at octave

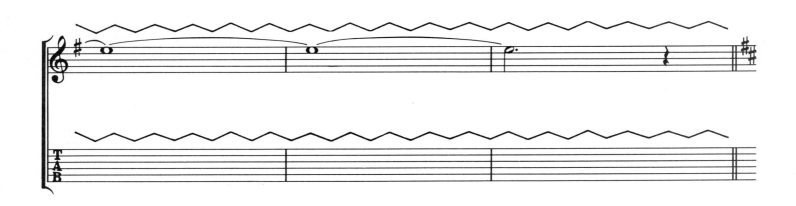

B5
8va -

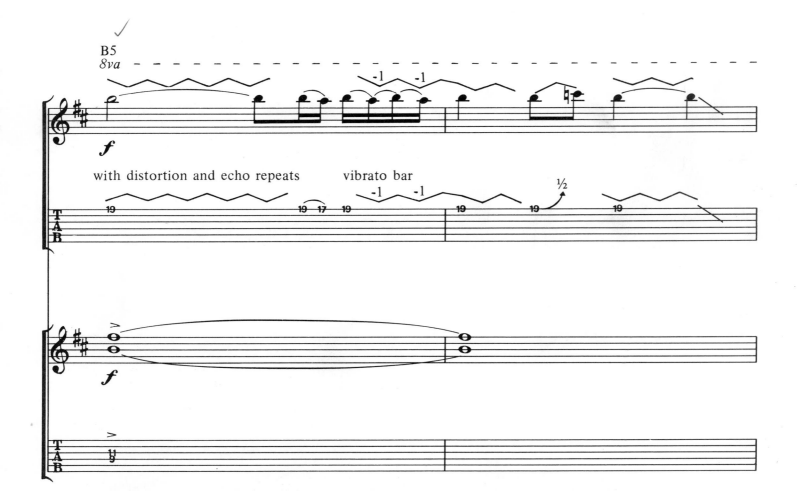

with distortion and echo repeats   vibrato bar

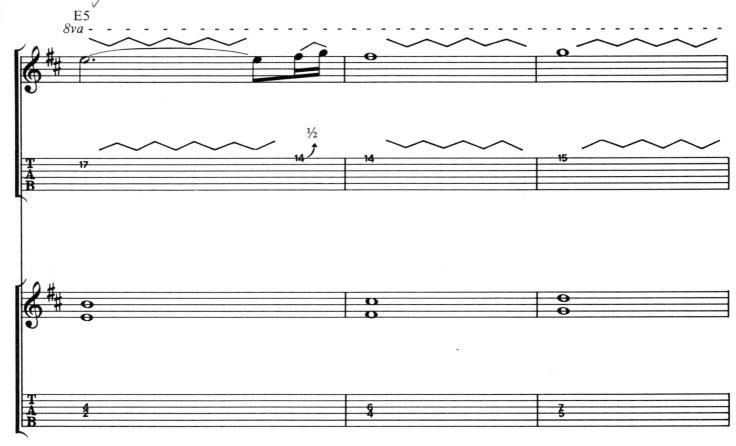

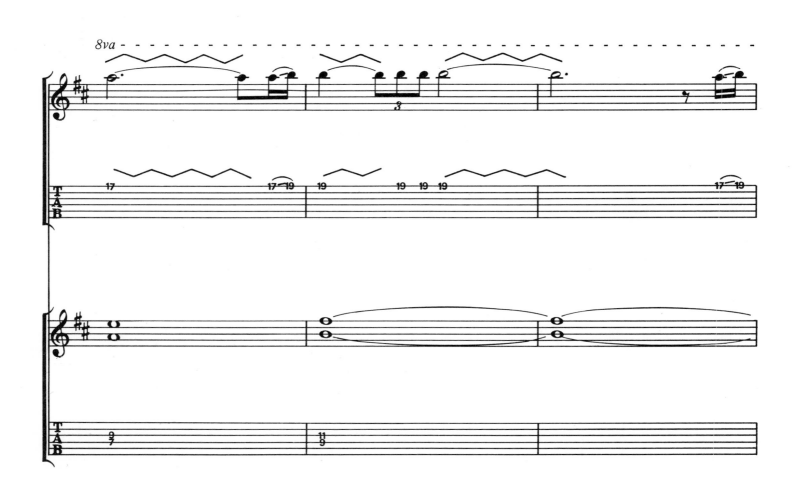

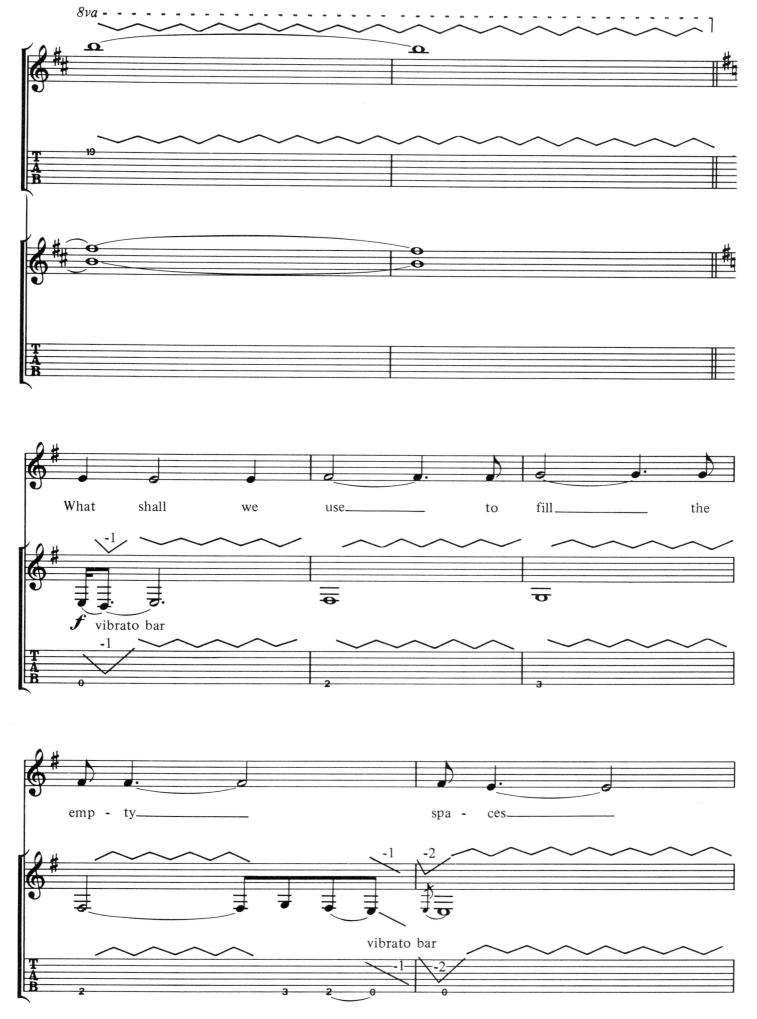

What shall we use_____ to fill_____ the

emp - ty_____ spa - ces_____

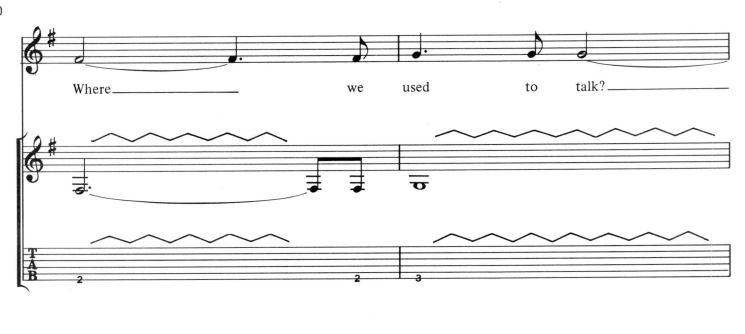

Where_____ we used to talk?_____

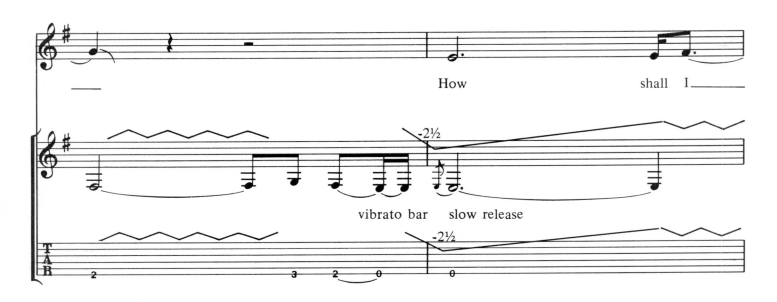

___ How shall I___

vibrato bar   slow release

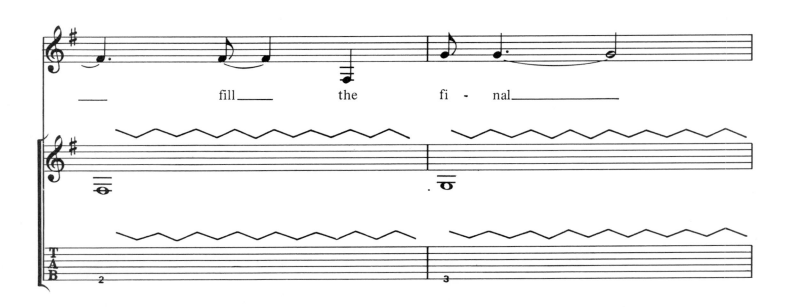

___ fill___ the fi - nal_____

pla - ces?　　　　　　　　　　　　　　　　　　　How　　should　I

vibrato bar　　slow, even release

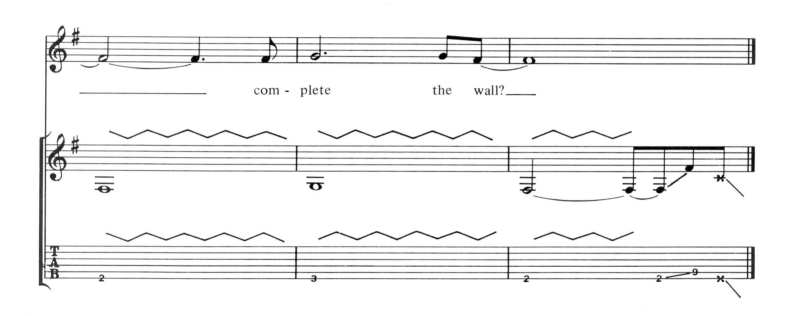

＿＿＿＿＿＿＿＿＿＿＿＿＿＿＿ com - plete　　　the　　wall?＿＿＿

Young Lust

Words by ROGER WATERS
Music by DAVID GILMOUR/ROGER WATERS

Moderately ♩ = 95
Verse 1
(E5)
N.C.

I am just— a new— boy,

electric guitar 1

let ring

stran - ger in this town.—

let ring
P.M.

with feedback at fifteenth

Where are all— the good— times?

let ring

P.H.

P.H.

Who's gon - na show this strang - er a - round.

Verse 2

Will some wom-an in this des-ert land

let ring

make me feel like a real man? Take this

let ring

Ooh,_____ I need a dir - ty

girl.

Guitar solo

P.M.

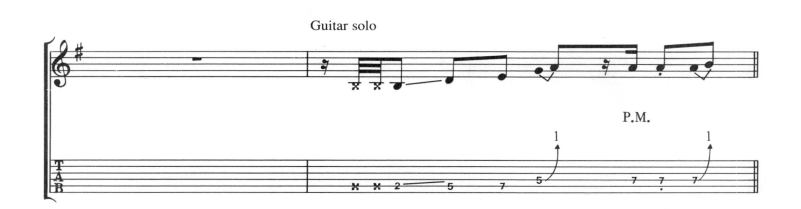

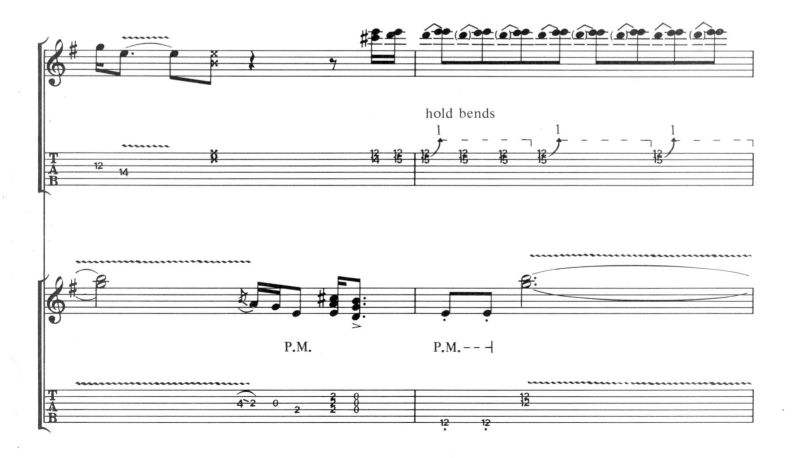

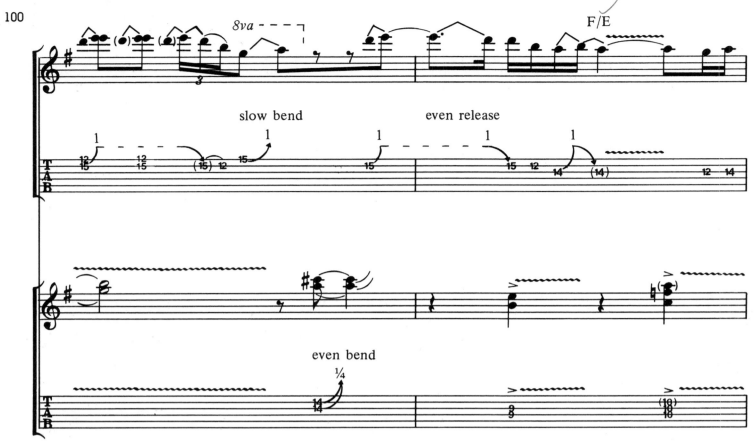

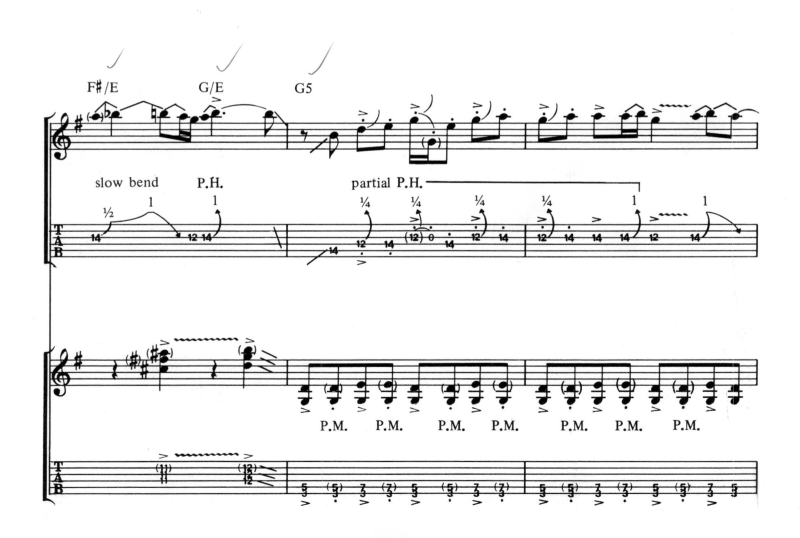

I need a dir - ty   girl.

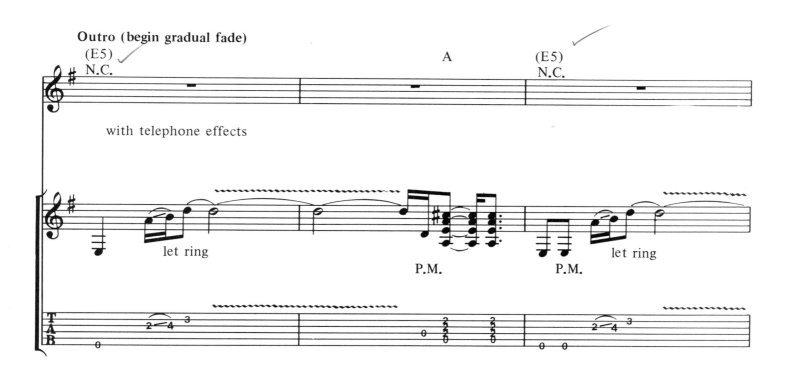

Outro (begin gradual fade)

with telephone effects

let ring   P.M.   P.M.   let ring

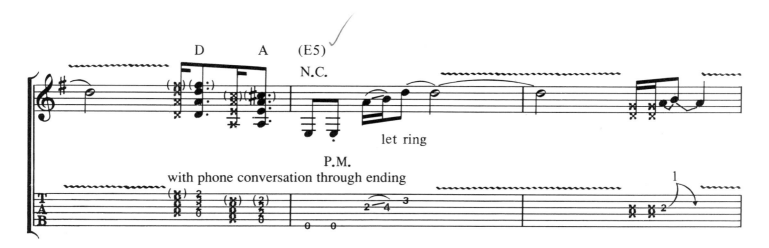

let ring

P.M.
with phone conversation through ending

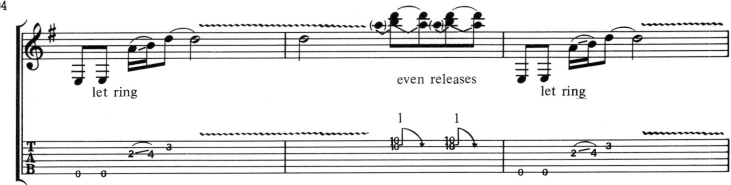

let ring

even releases

let ring

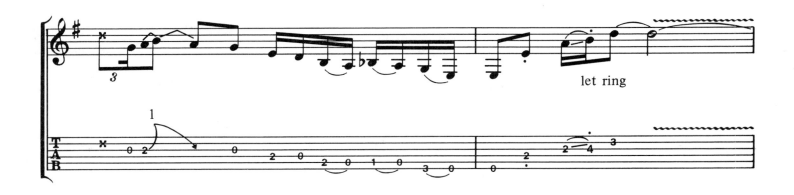

let ring

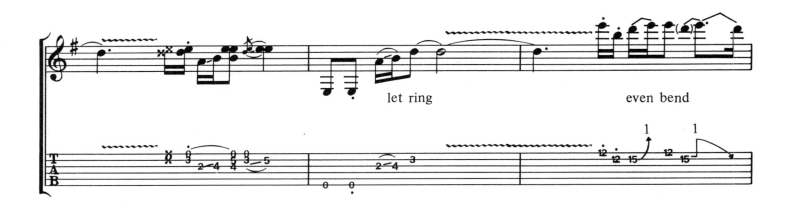

let ring

even bend

E5

Segue to "One of My Turns"

Operator: "This is the United States calling. Are we reaching?" (click)

"See, he keeps hanging up,
And it's a man answering."
(dial tone)

One of My Turns

Moderately ♩ = 110

guitar tacet

Words & Music by
ROGER WATERS

girl's voice with television sound effects
and synthesizer drone for approximately
45 seconds

Day af - ter day, love turns grey,

like the skin of_____ a dy - ing_____ man._

And night af - ter night, we pre - tend it's all right,_

but I have grown old - er,_____ and you have_ grown_

cold - er,_ and noth - ing_____ is ver - y_ much_ fun_____ an - y - more,_

_ and I can feel_____

one of_ my_ turns com - ing on. I

feel_____ cold as a ra - zor blade,_ tight as a

tour - ni - quet,_ dry as a fu - ner - al_ drum.

ritard.

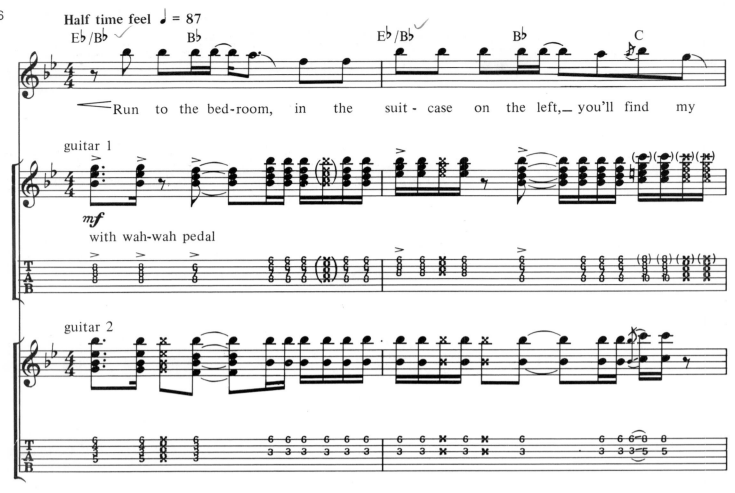

Run to the bed-room, in the suit-case on the left,— you'll find my

fav - or - ite axe.—

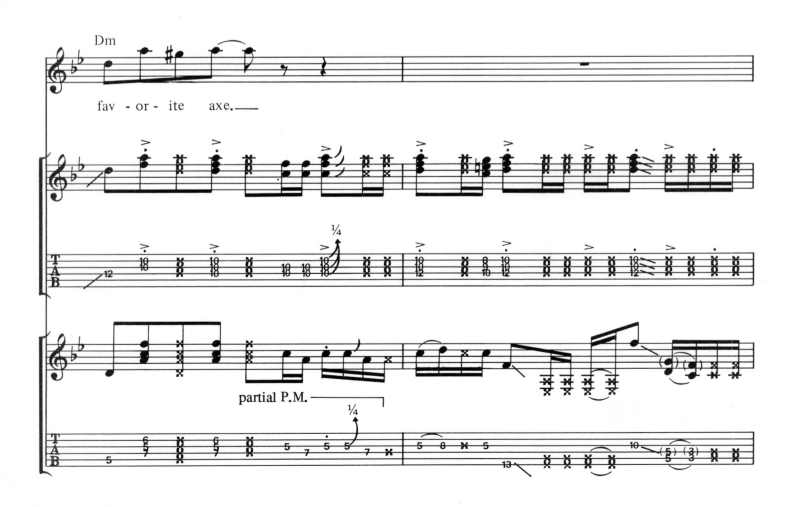

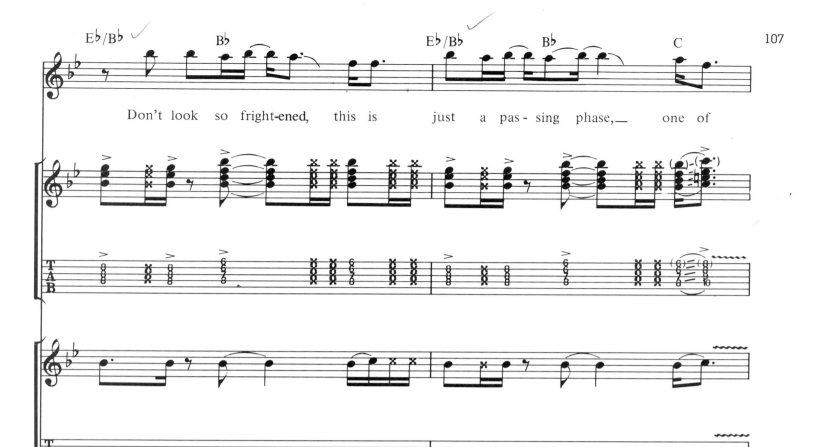

Don't look so fright-ened, this is just a pas-sing phase,— one of

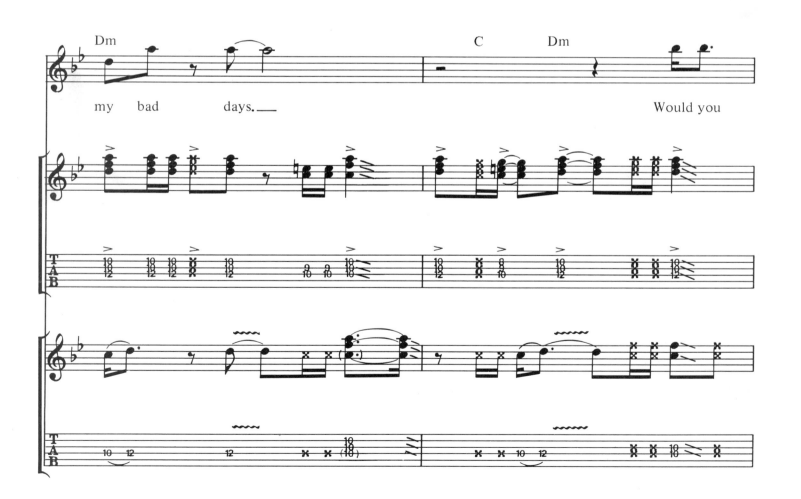

my bad days.— Would you

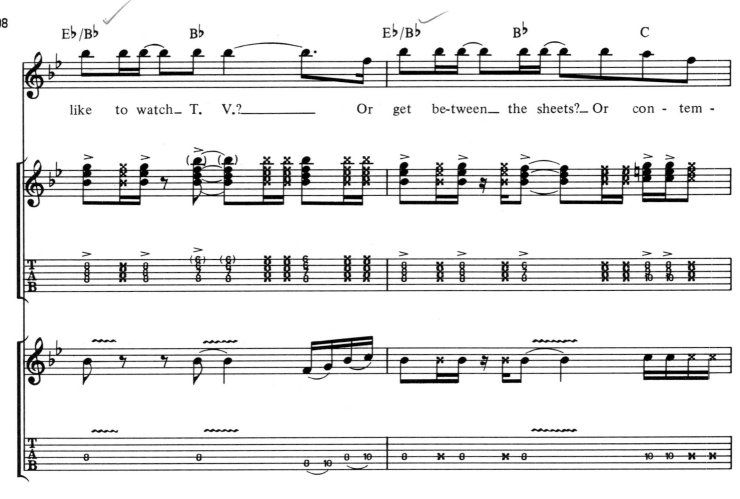

like to watch T. V.? Or get be-tween the sheets? Or con - tem -

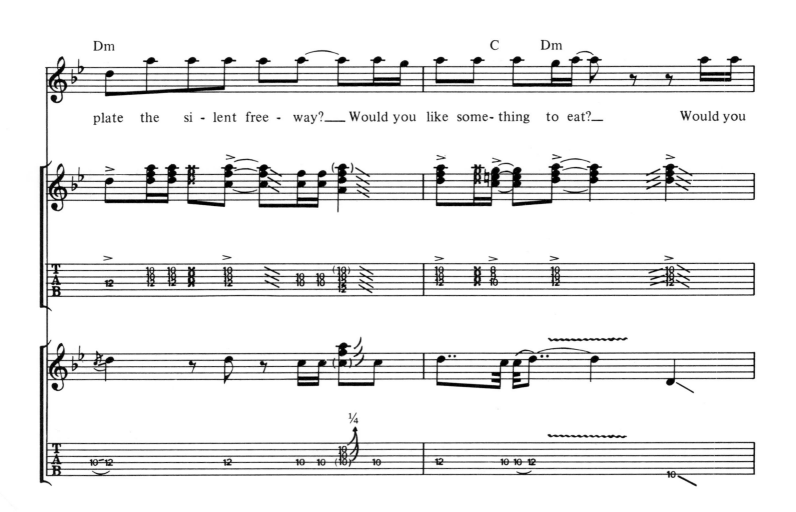

plate the si - lent free - way? Would you like some-thing to eat? Would you

like to learn to fly? — Would you?— Would you

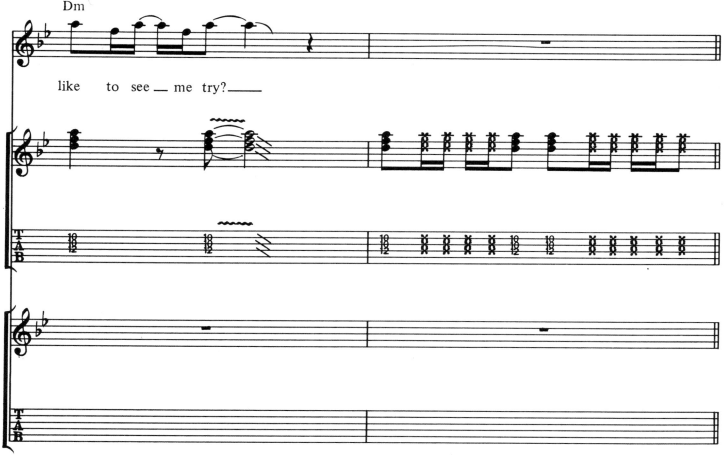

like to see — me try?—

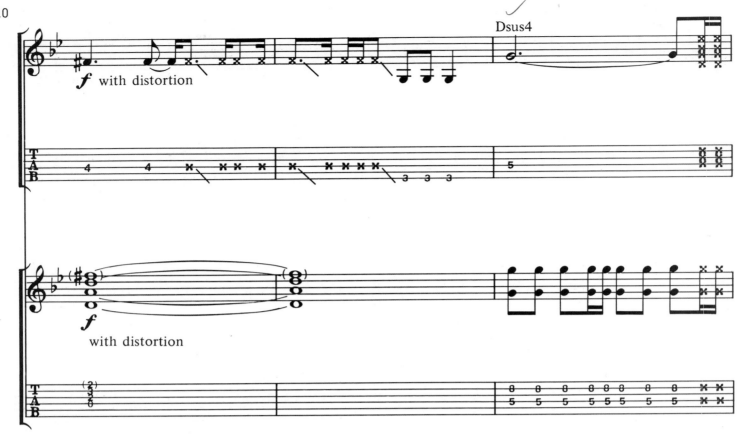

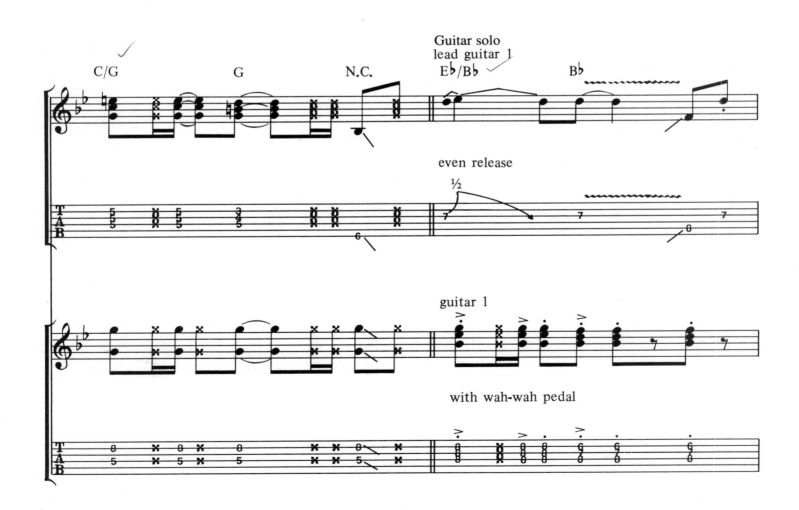

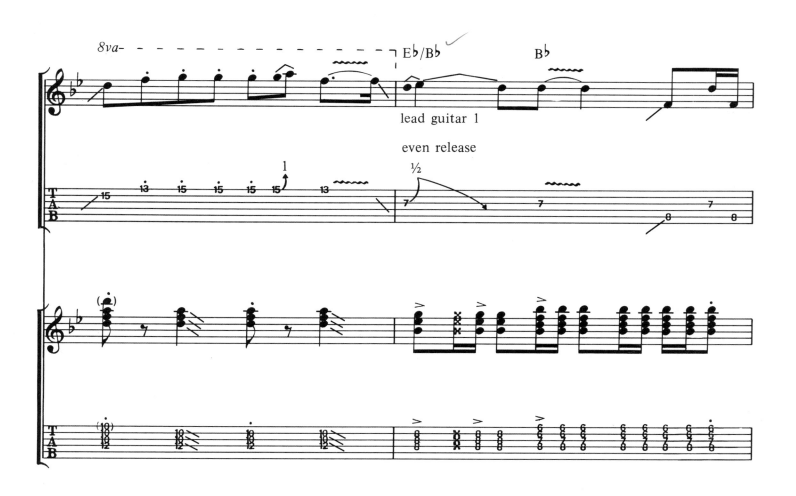

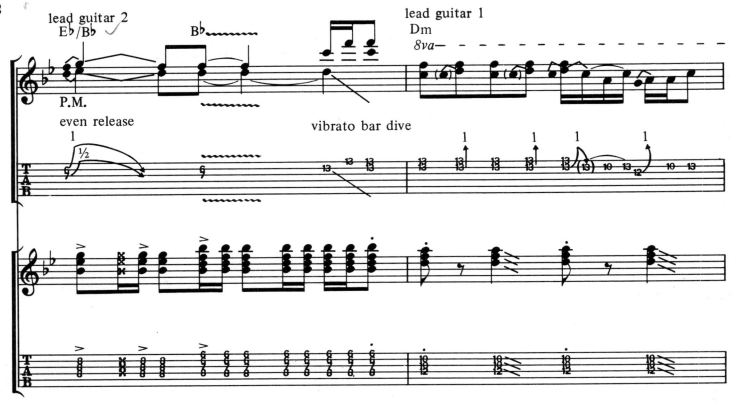

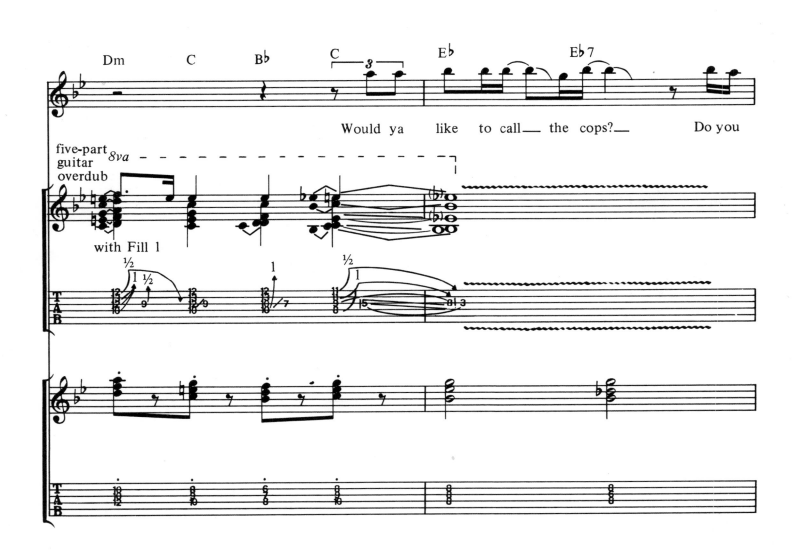

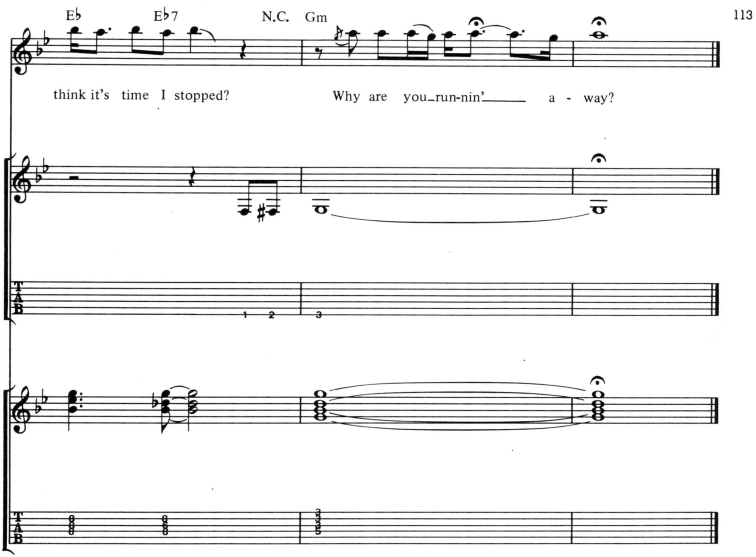

think it's time I stopped? Why are you run-nin'_____ a - way?

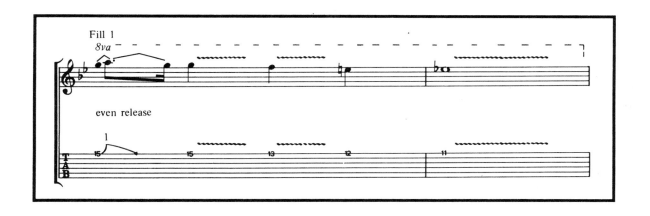

Fill 1
8va

even release

Don't Leave me now

Words & Music by
ROGER WATERS

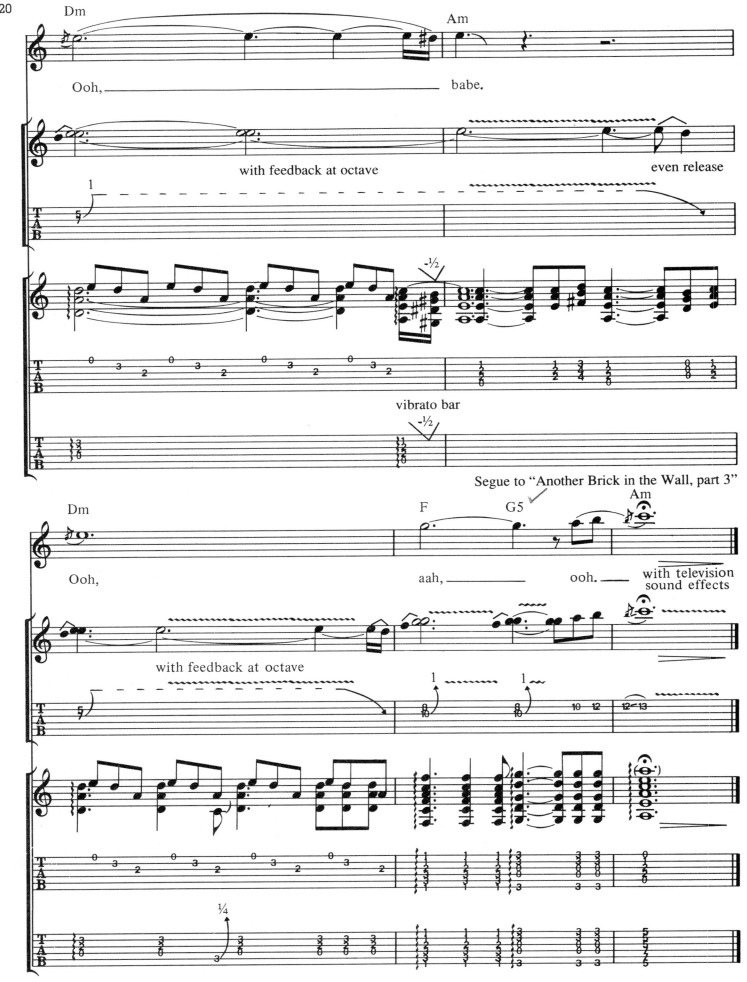

Another Brick in the Wall. part 3.

Words & Music by
ROGER WATERS

And I don't need ___ no

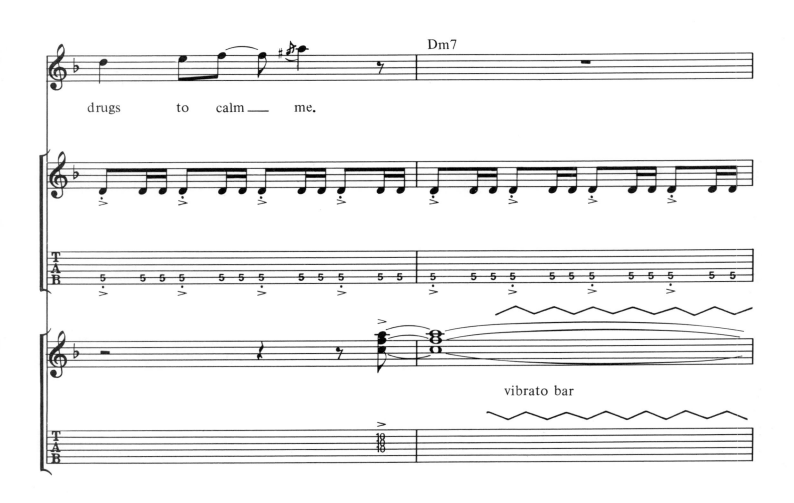

drugs to calm ___ me.

vibrato bar

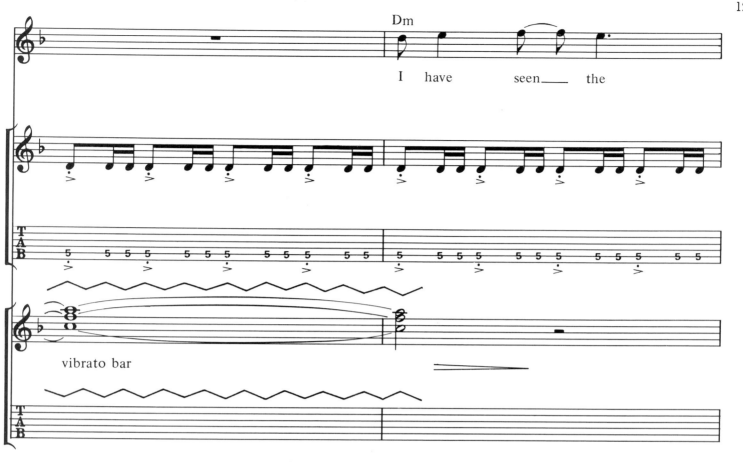

I have seen___ the

vibrato bar

writ - ing on ___ the wall. ___

Don't think I _____ need

vibrato bar

G

an - y thing ___ at all. ___

with Rhythm fill 1 (4 times)

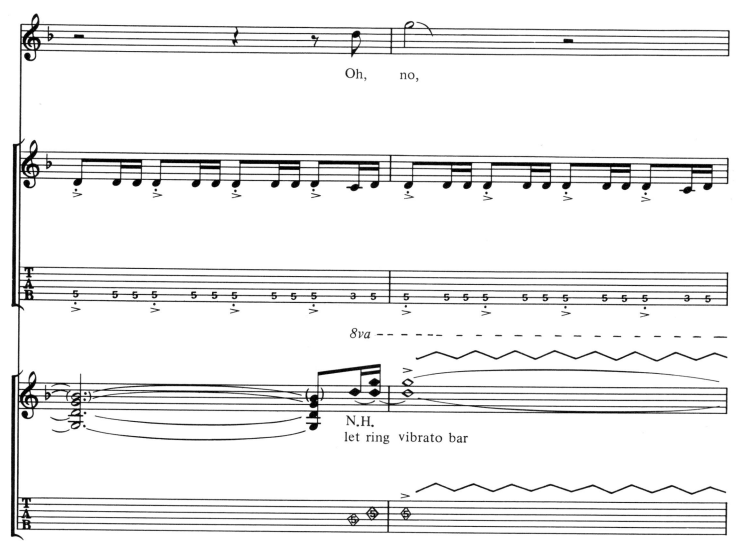

Oh,   no,

N.H.
let ring vibrato bar

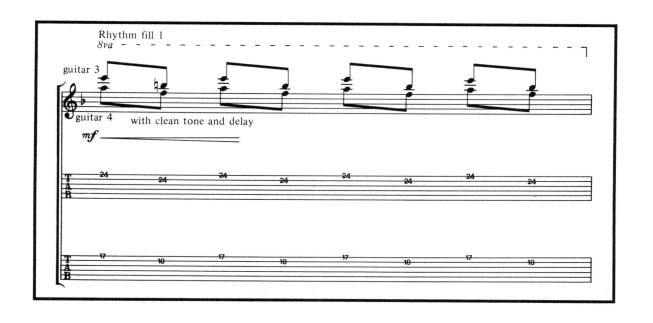

Rhythm fill 1
8va - - - - - - - - - - - -

guitar 3

guitar 4 with clean tone and delay

mf

don't think I'll need an - y - thing __ at all. __

8va

let ring

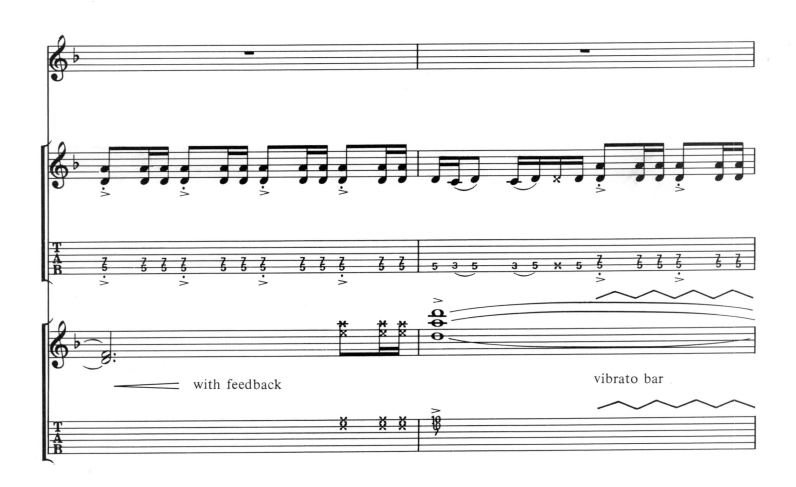

with feedback

vibrato bar

All in all— you were _____

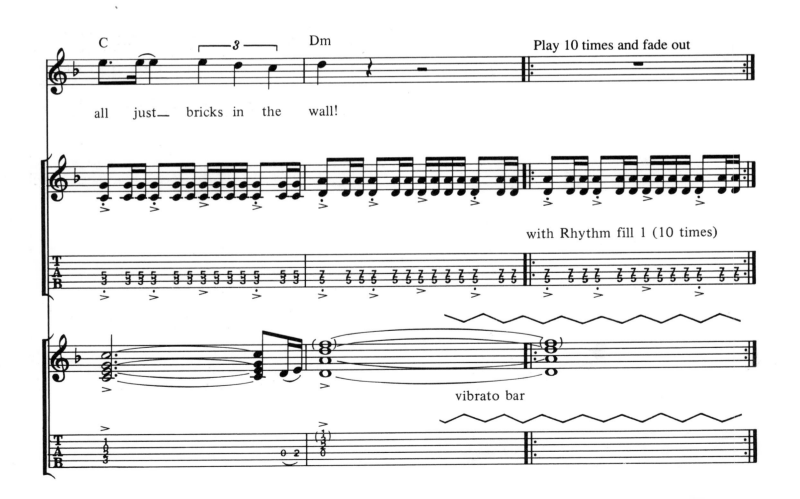

C — 3 — Dm Play 10 times and fade out

all just— bricks in the wall!

with Rhythm fill 1 (10 times)

vibrato bar

Goodbye Cruel World

Words & Music by
ROGER WATERS

Slowly

Good-bye, cruel world, I'm leav-ing you to-day. — Good-bye, — Good-bye, — Good-bye.

Good-bye, all you peo-ple, — There's noth-ing you can say To make me change my mind. — Good-bye.

Hey you

Words & Music by
ROGER WATERS

Moderately with half-time feel ♩ = 112
Intro
acoustic steel string guitar 1 (Capo 3rd fret)

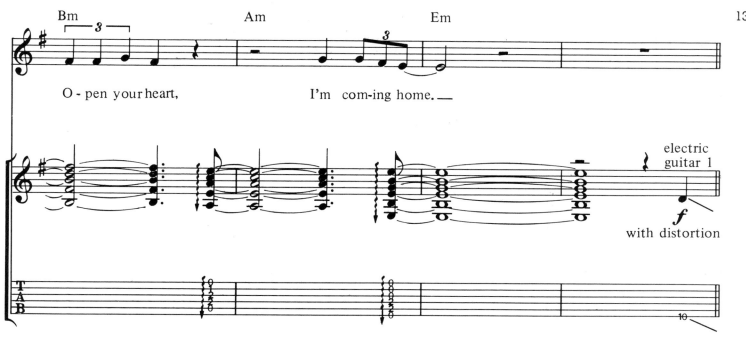

O - pen your heart,   I'm com-ing home. __

Guitar solo
electric guitar 2

Solo figure 1

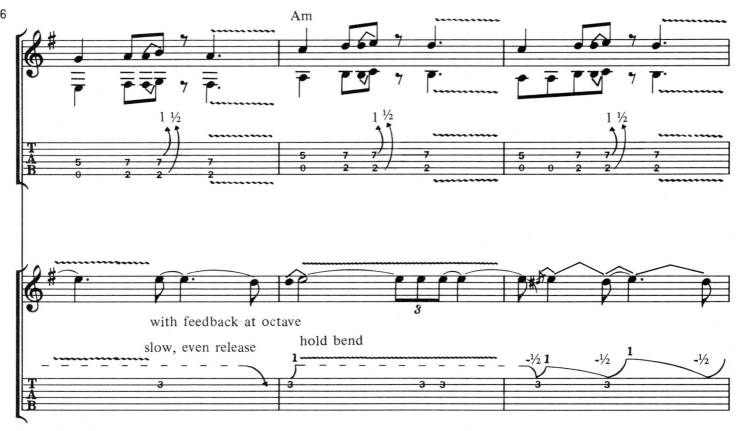

with feedback at octave

slow, even release   hold bend

electric slide guitar
Em

end Solo
figure 1   with Solo figure 1 (2 times)

steady gliss

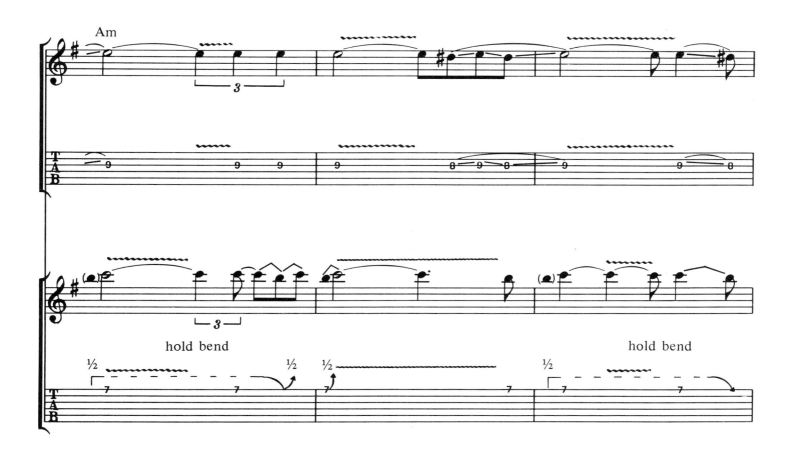

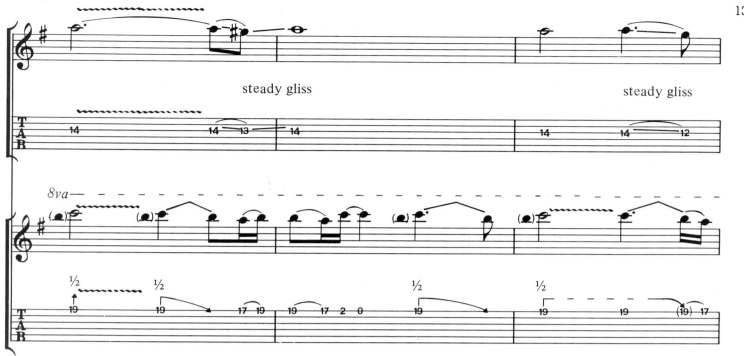

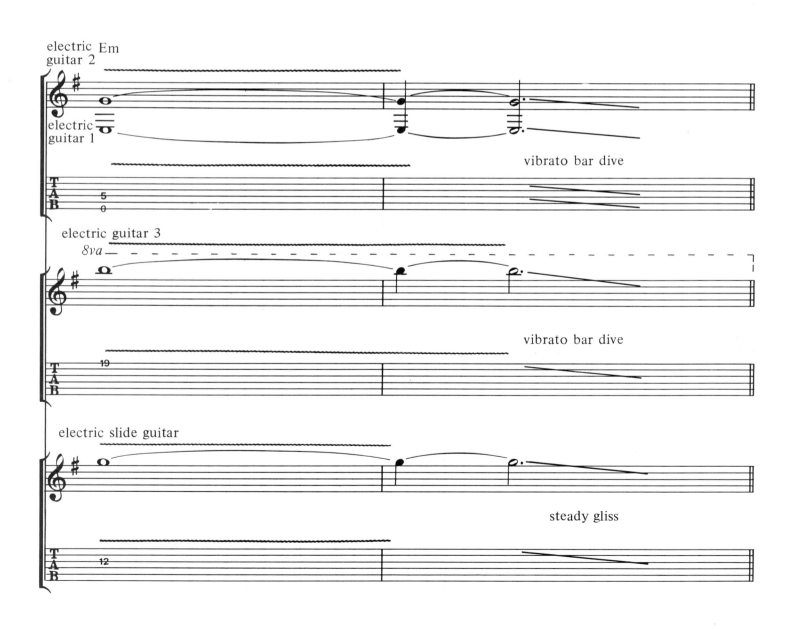

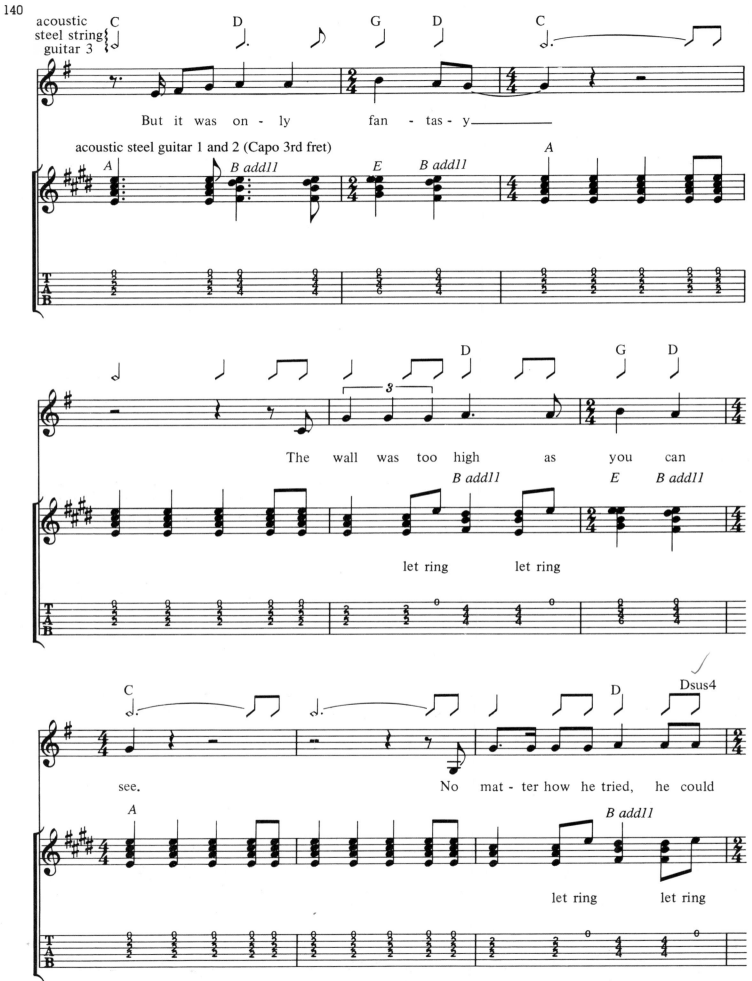

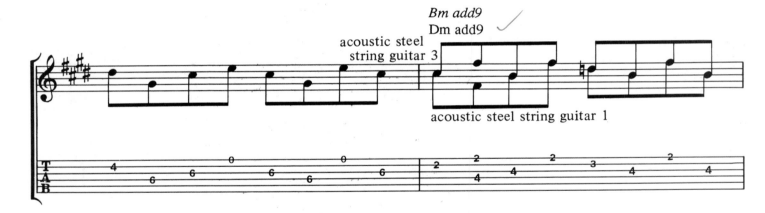

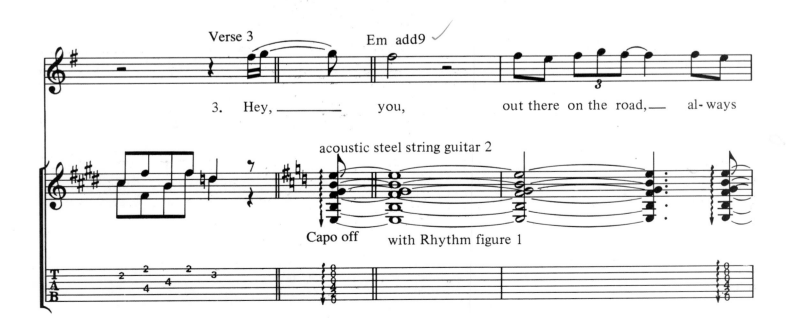

3. Hey, _____ you, out there on the road,— al- ways

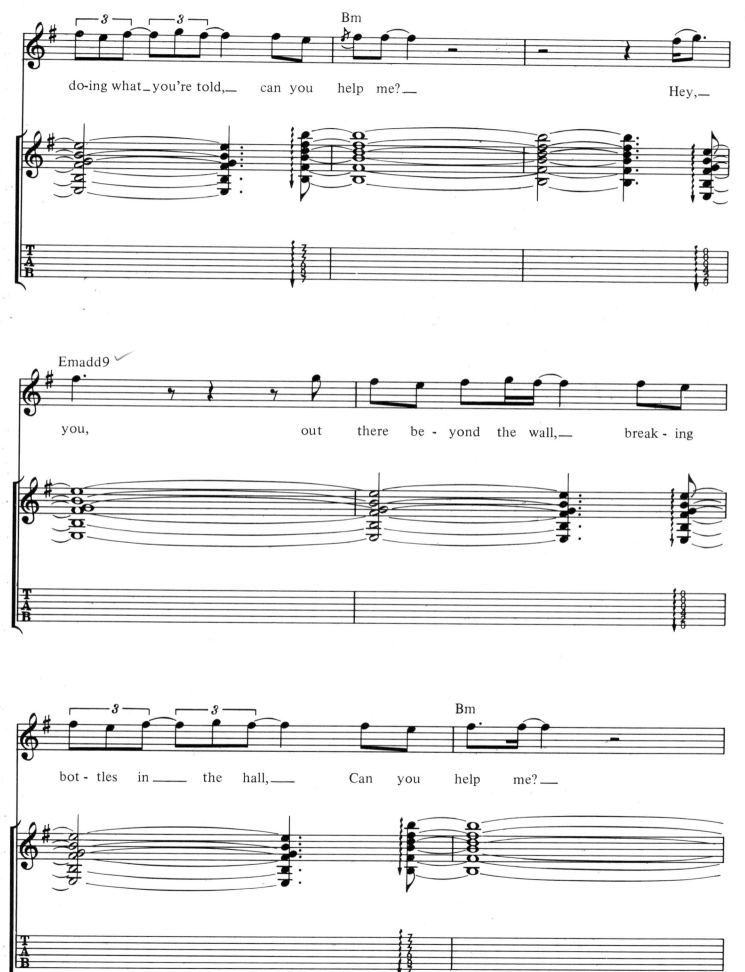

144

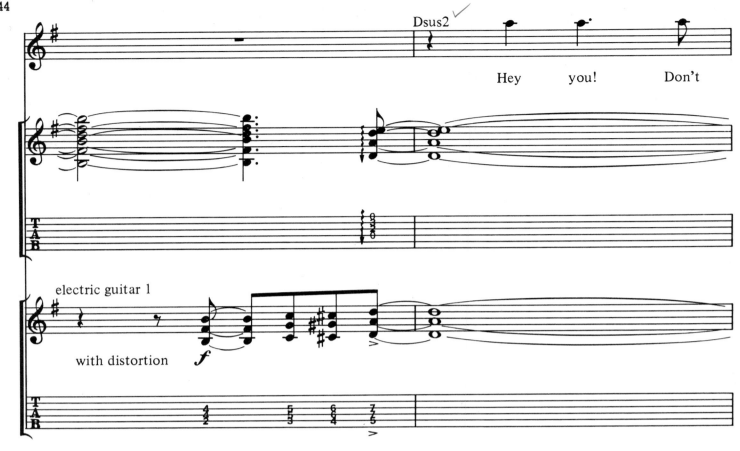

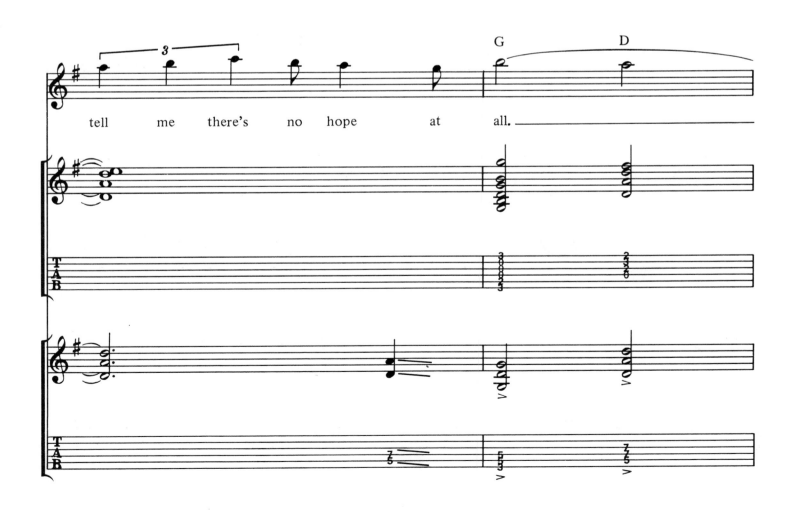

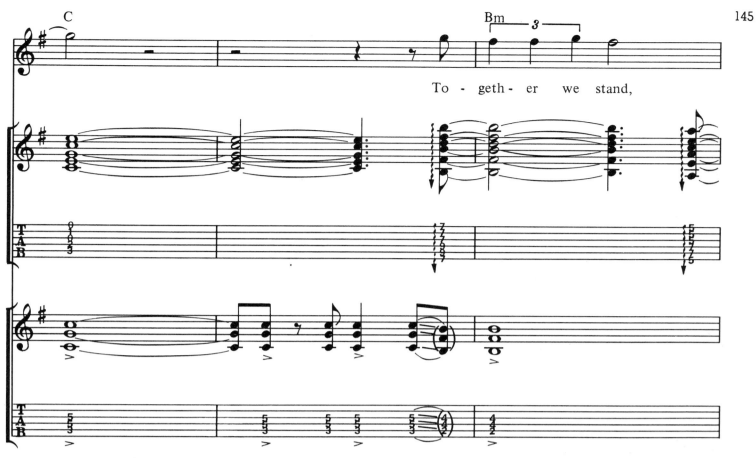

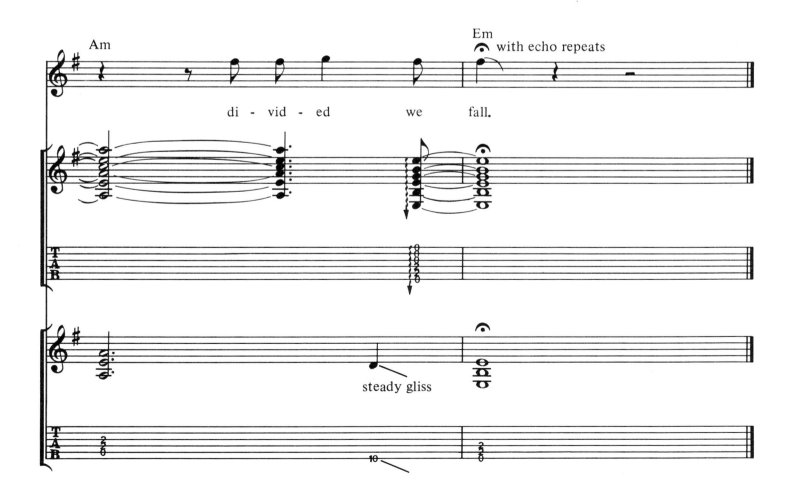

Is there anybody out there?

Words & Music by
ROGER WATERS

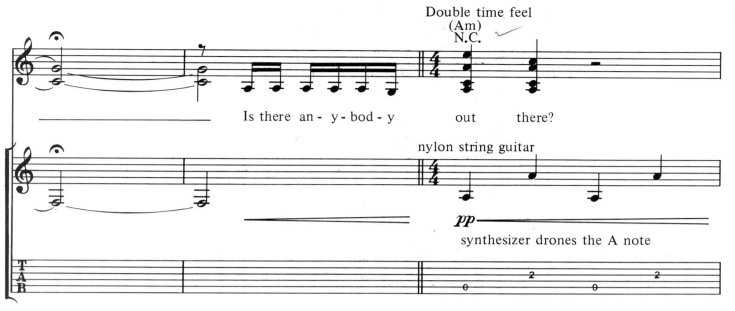

Is there an - y - bod - y out there?

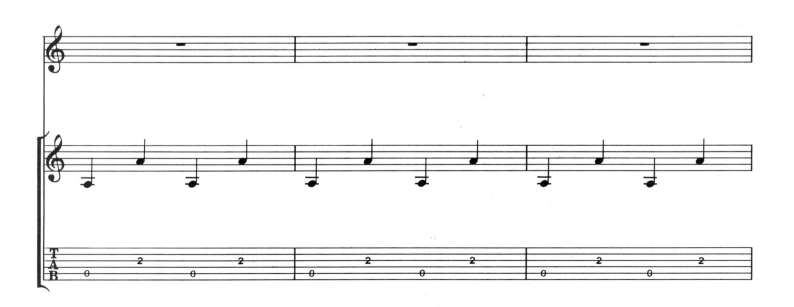

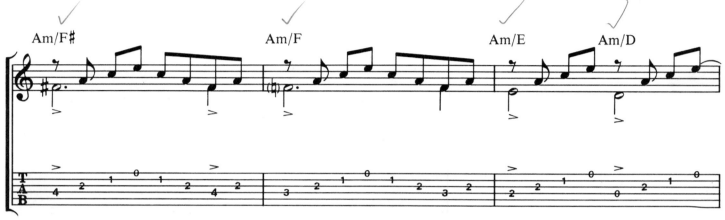

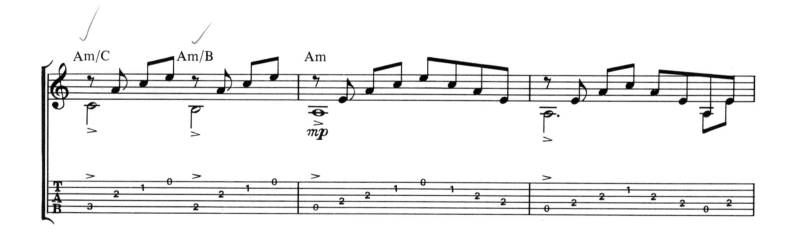

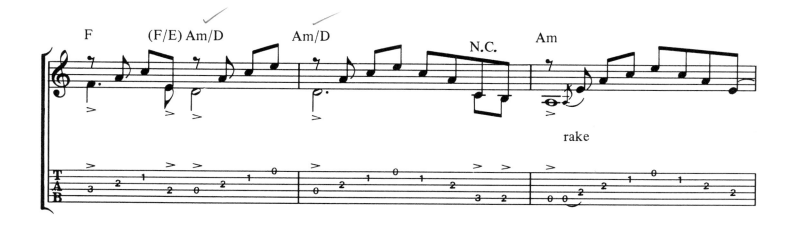

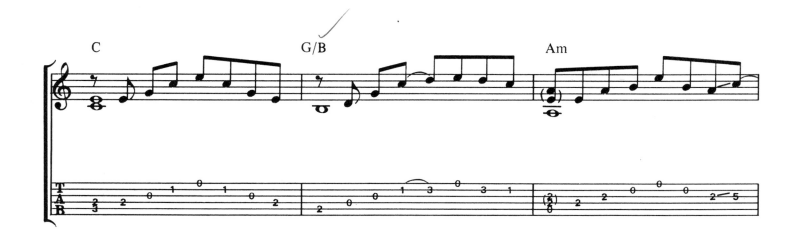

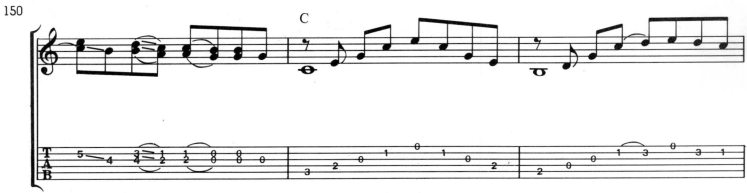

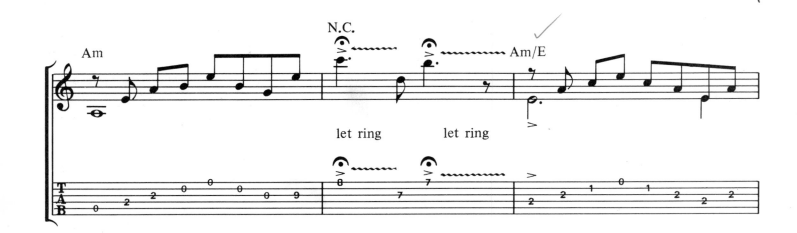

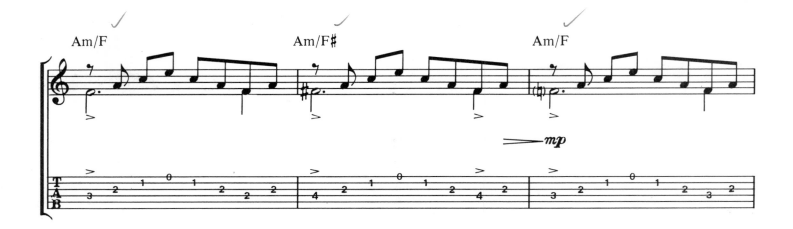

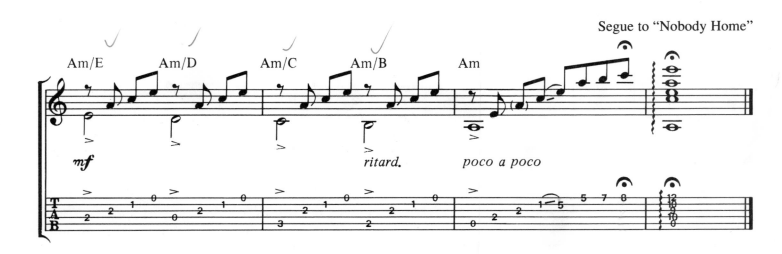

Nobody Home

Words & Music by
ROGER WATERS

I've got the ob-lig-a-to-ry—— Hendrix perm—— And the in-ev-i-ta-ble—— pin-hole

burns   All   down the front   of my   fav-our-ite   sa-tin   shirt.——

—— I've got   nic-o-tine stains   on my   fin-gers,—— I've got a   sil-ver spoon   on a

chain.——   I've got   a   grand   pi-an-o   to   prop up my   mor-tal   re-mains.——

—— I've got   wild   star-ing   eyes   And I've got a strong urge to

Vera

Words & Music by
ROGER WATERS

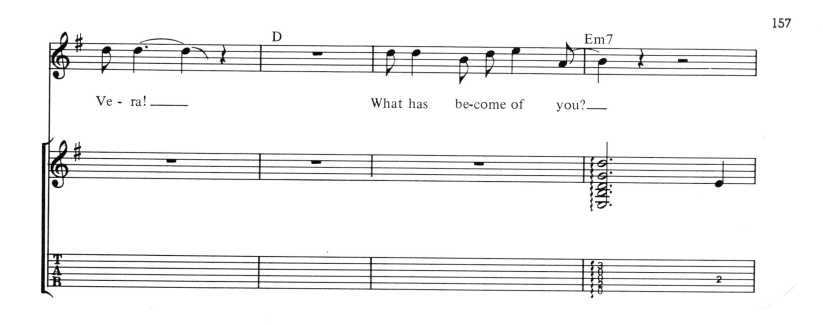

Ve - ra! ____ What has be-come of you?____

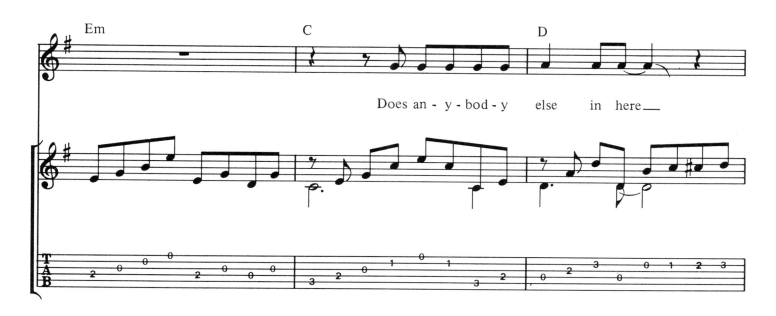

Does an - y - bod - y else in here____

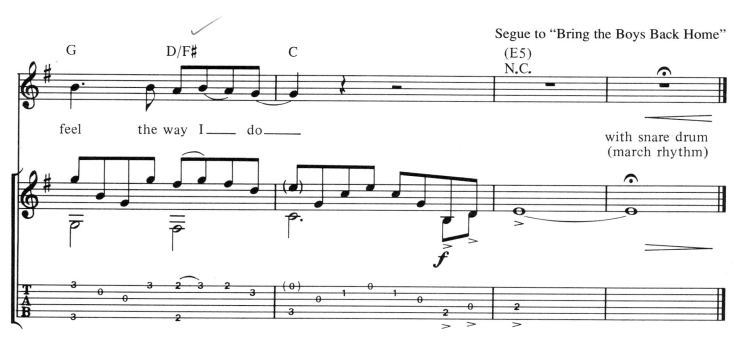

feel the way I ____ do____

Segue to "Bring the Boys Back Home"

(E5)
N.C.

with snare drum
(march rhythm)

Bring the boys back home

Words & Music by
ROGER WATERS

Comfortably Numb

Words by ROGER WATERS
Music by DAVID GILMOUR/ROGER WATERS

an-y-one-home? Come on now,— I hear you're feel-ing down,— well,

I can ease your pain— and get you on your feet a-gain.—

Re-lax, I'll need some in-for-ma-tion first,

with slide guitar fill 1

just the ba - sic facts,——— Can you show me where it hurts?

Pre-chorus

There is— no pain——you are— re - ced - ing.—

acoustic guitar

Rhythm figure 1 (keyboard arranged for guitar)

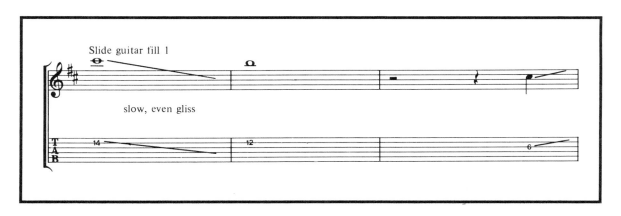

Slide guitar fill 1

slow, even gliss

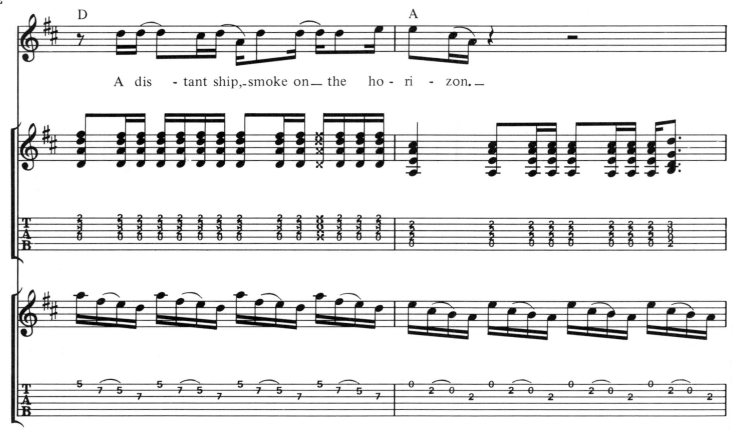

A dis - tant ship, smoke on the ho - ri - zon.

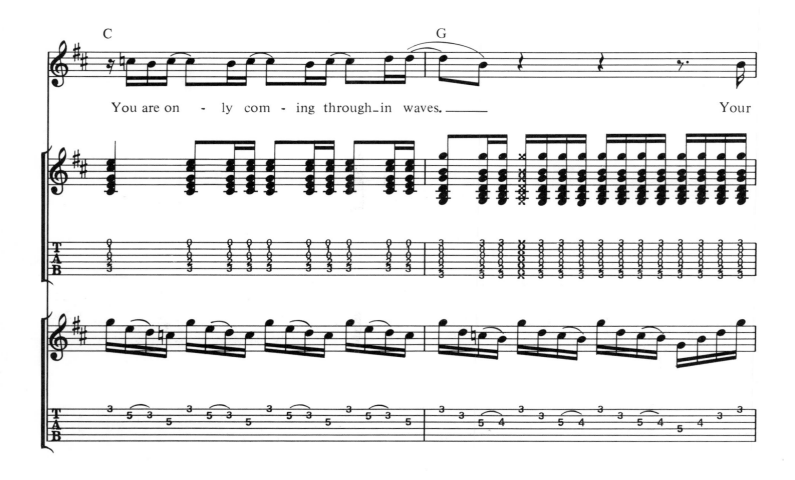

You are on - ly com - ing through in waves. Your

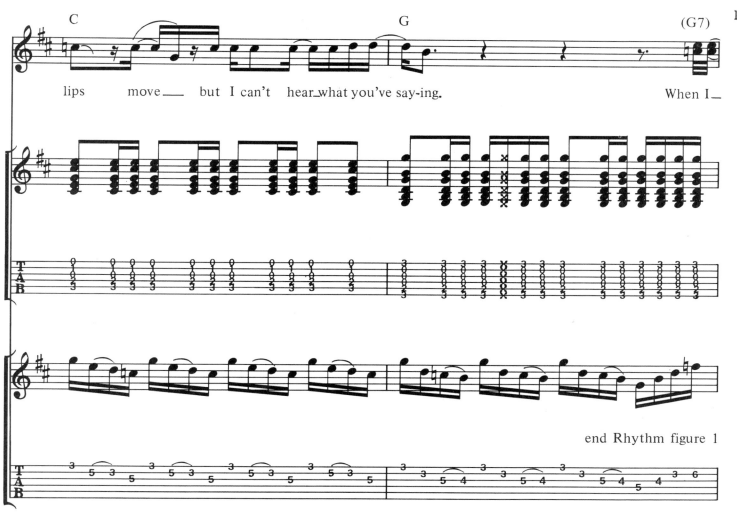

end Rhythm figure 1

lips   move___ but I can't   hear___what you've say-ing.

When I___

___   was a child,   I ___had a fe - ver.___

My

with Rhythm figure 1

hands felt—just like— two— bal-loons.—

Now I've got— that feel - ing once— a - gain.— I can't ex-plain, you would not un-

— der stand.— This is not how— I am.

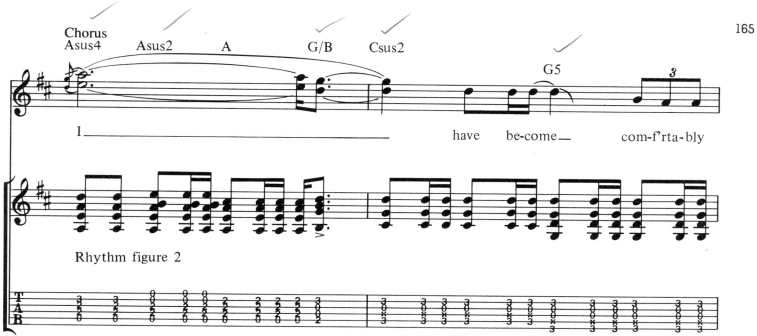

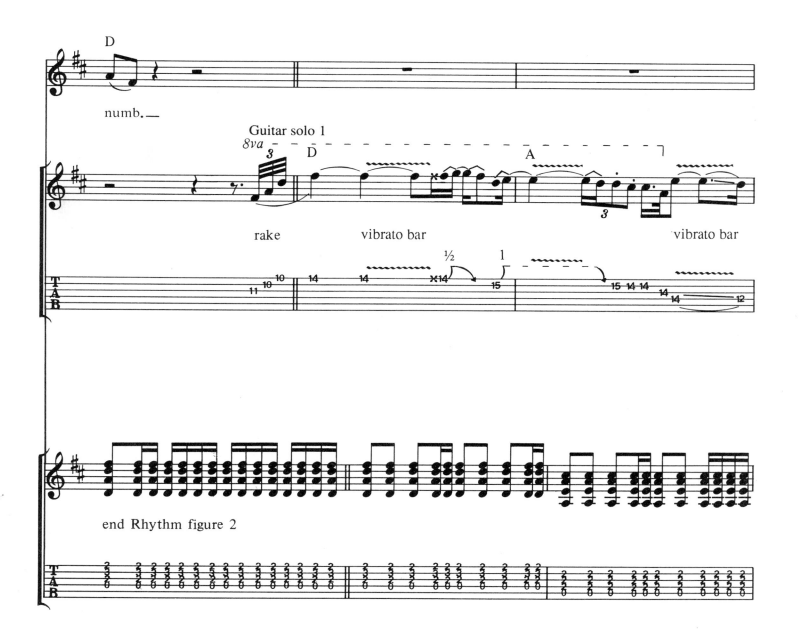

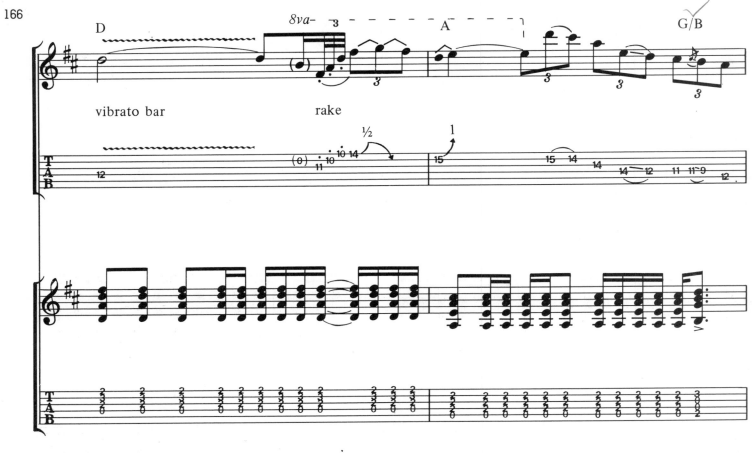

vibrato bar   rake

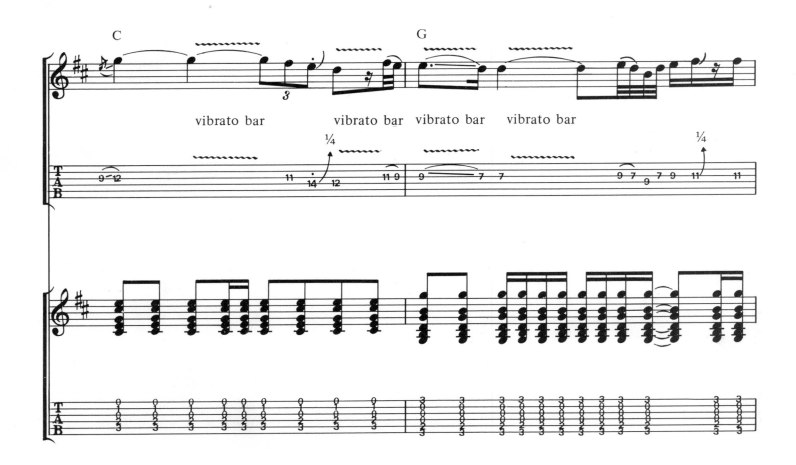

vibrato bar   vibrato bar   vibrato bar   vibrato bar

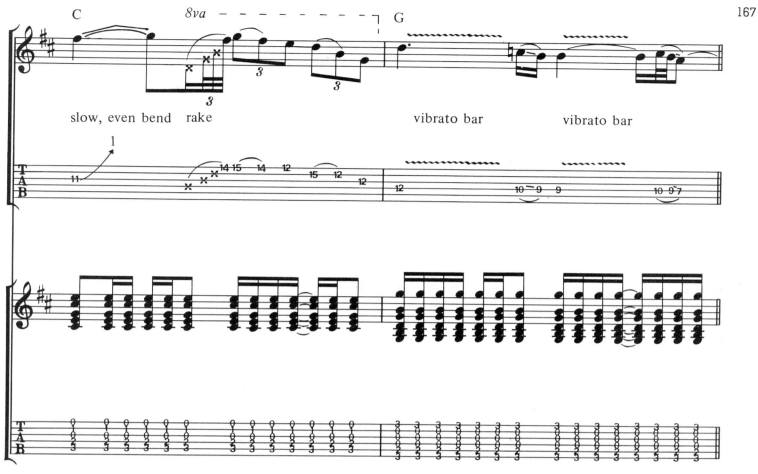

slow, even bend   rake   vibrato bar   vibrato bar

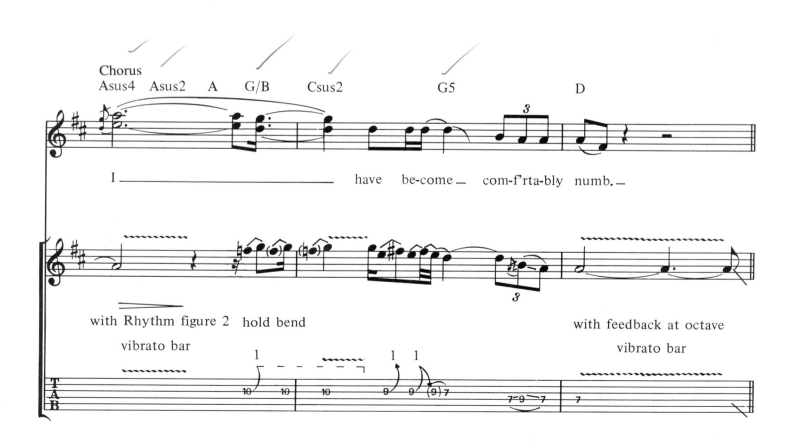

Chorus
Asus4 Asus2 A G/B Csus2   G5   D

I _____ have be-come— com-f'rta-bly numb.—

with Rhythm figure 2 hold bend   with feedback at octave
vibrato bar   vibrato bar

go-ing   through the show,— come on, it's time to go.

Pre-chorus (with Rhythm figure 1)

There is ___ no pain___ you are___ re - ced - ing. ___

A dis - tant ship,—smoke on ___ the ho - ri - zon. ___

You are on - ly com - ing through ___ in ___ waves. ___ Your

lips move— but I can't hear what you're say-ing. When I was a child I caught a

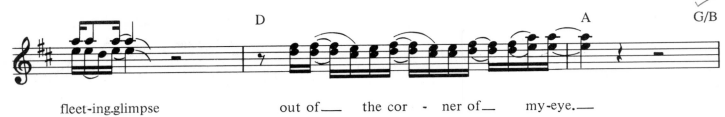

fleet-ing.glimpse out of the cor - ner of my-eye.

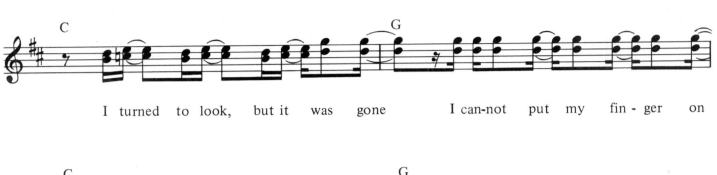

I turned to look, but it was gone I can-not put my fin - ger on

_ it now. _ The child is grown, _ the dream is gone. _

(use for last bar of Rhythm figure 1)

Chorus
Asus4 Asus2 A G/B Csus2 G5 D

I_____ have be-come ____com-f'rta-bly numb. _

with Rhythm figure 2

electric guitar

divisi

A.H.
with
distortion

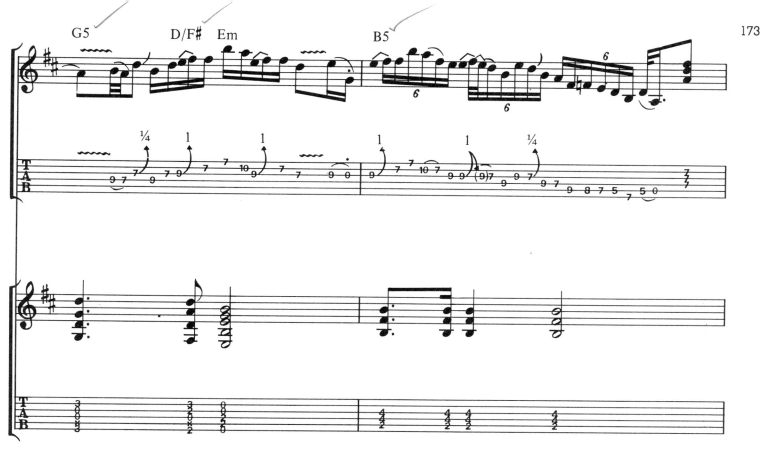

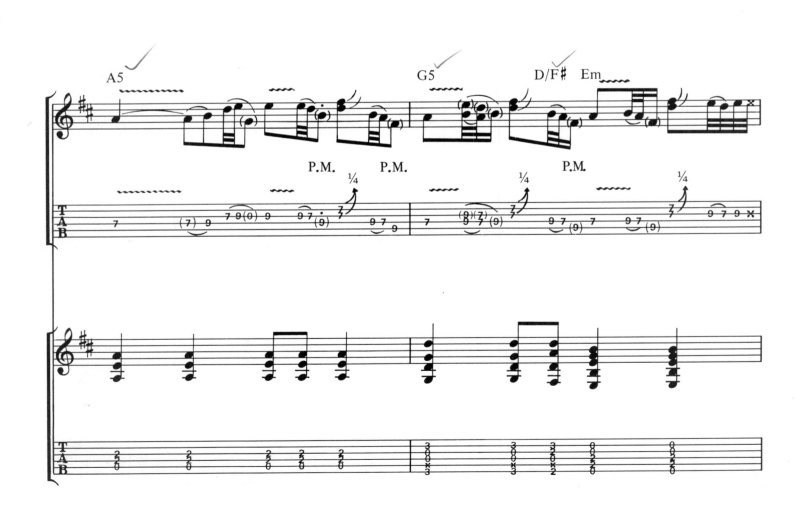

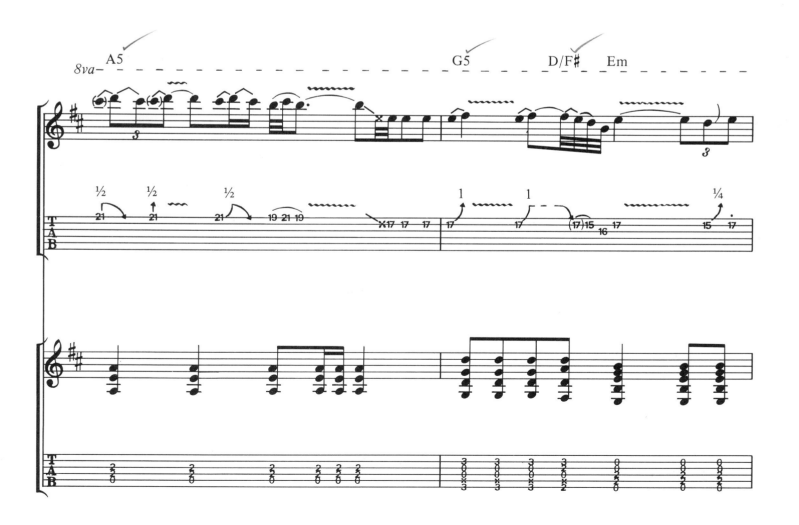

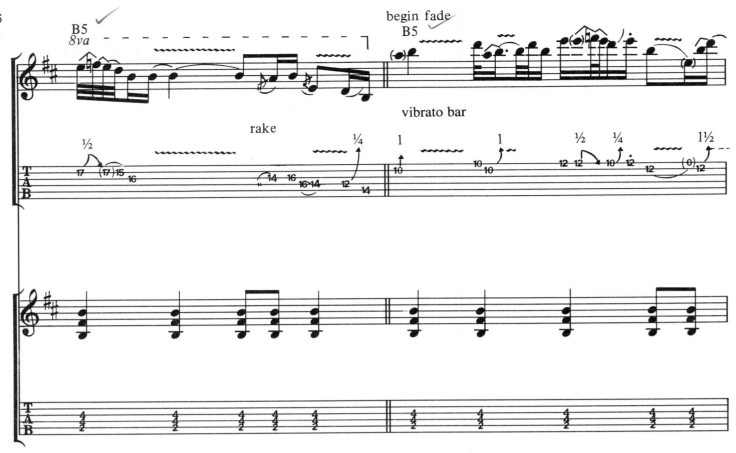

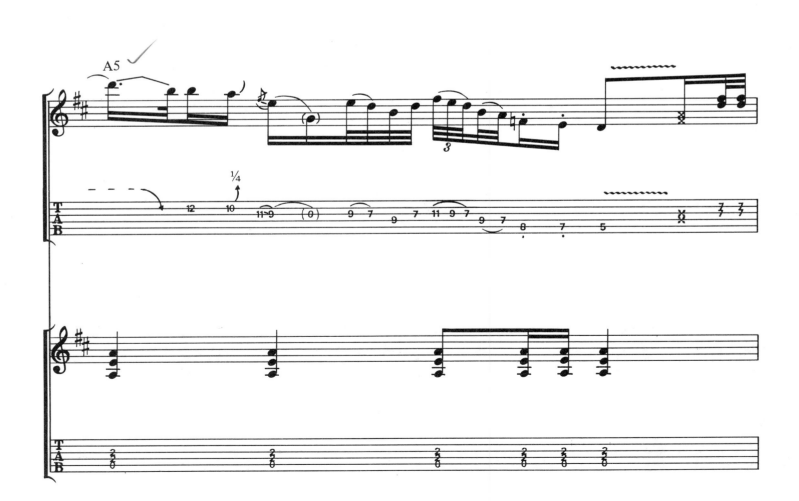

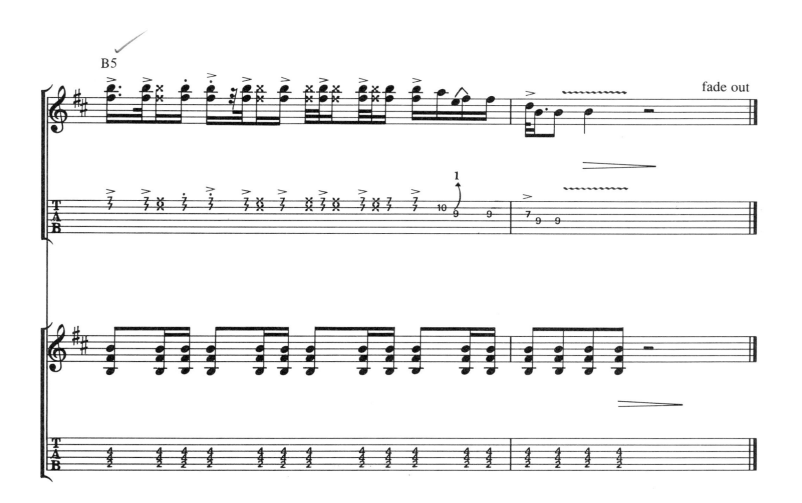

The Show must go on.

Words & Music by
ROGER WATERS

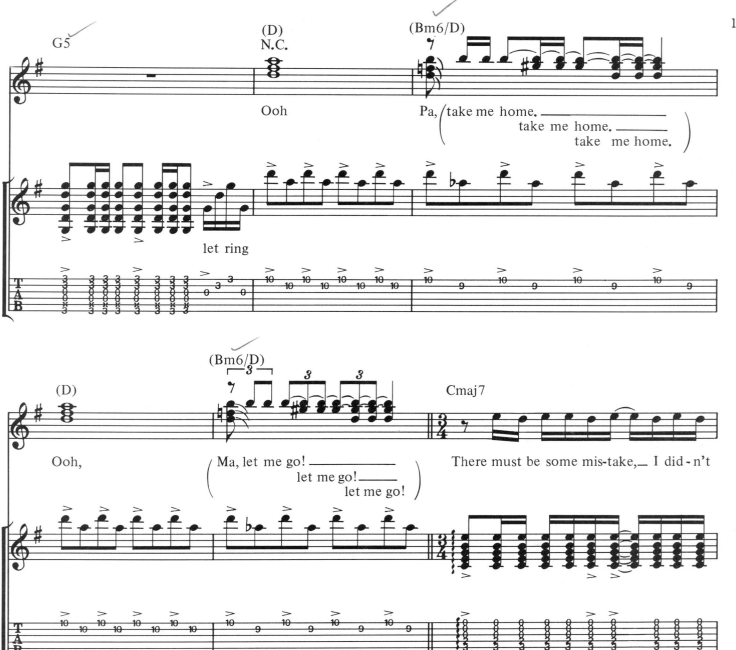

Words & Music by
ROGER WATERS

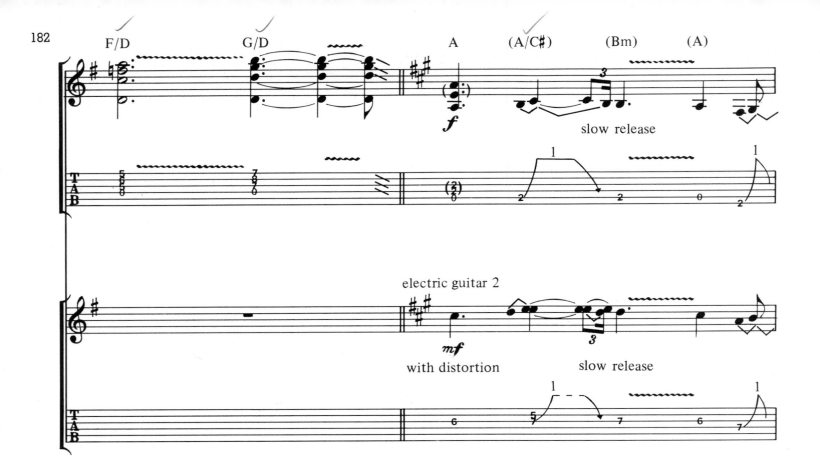

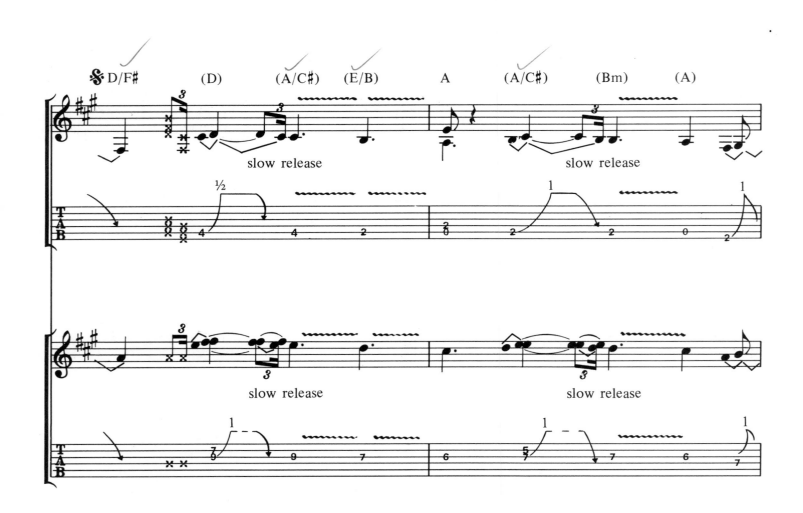

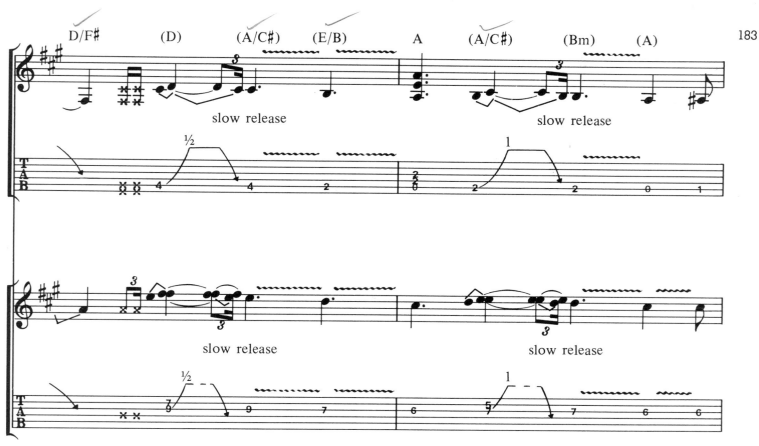

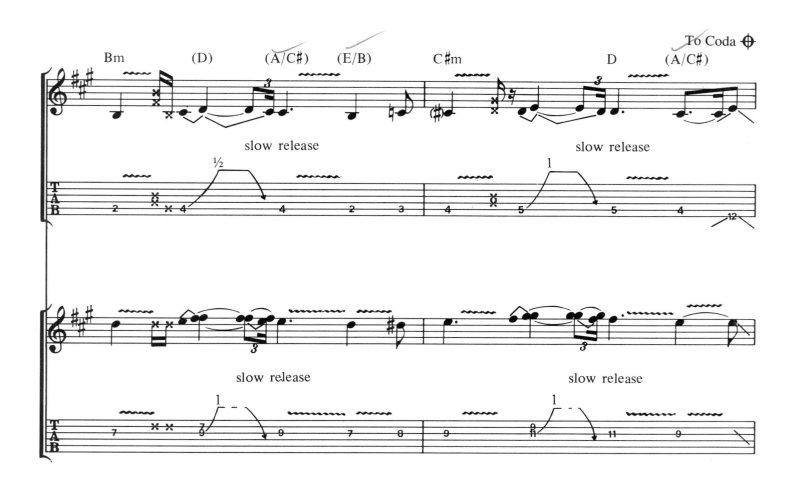

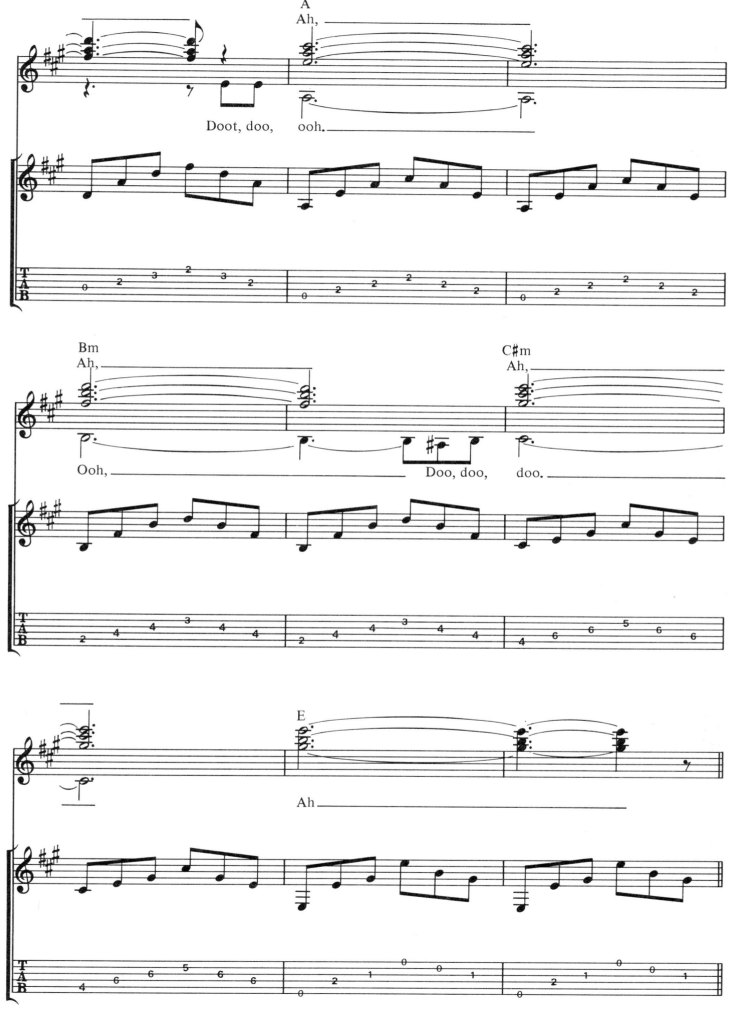

Verse 1

So ya thought ya might like to go to the show,___

let ring throughout

to feel the warm thrill of con - fu - sion, that

space – ca - det glow. I've got some bad

news   for you, sun-shine.   Pink is-n't well.___ He stayed back   at the hot - el   and they've

sent us a-long   as a   sur-ro-gate band.___   We're gon - na find   out where you

fans real - ly   stand.___   Are there   an-y queers   in the thea-tre to-night?   Get 'em

188

up a-gainst the wall.

(Choir:) Get them all!

There's one in the spot-light. He don't

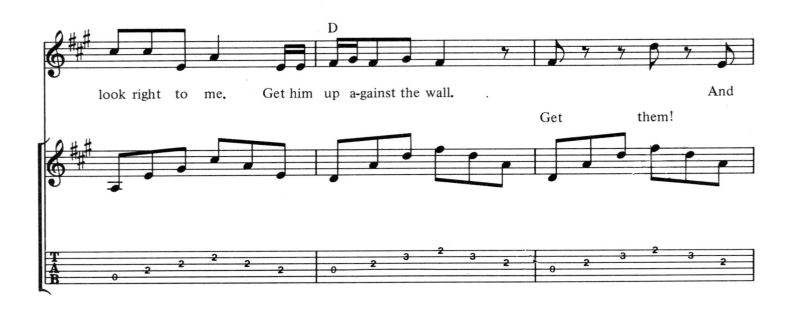

look right to me. Get him up a-gainst the wall.

Get them!

And

that one looks Jew-ish,— and that one's a coon.— Who let all this riff raff—

Run like Hell.

Words by ROGER WATERS
Music by DAVID GILMOUR/ROGER WATERS

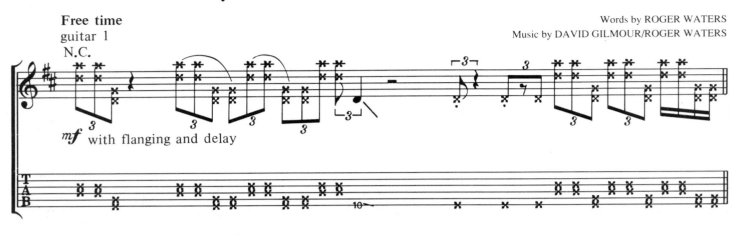

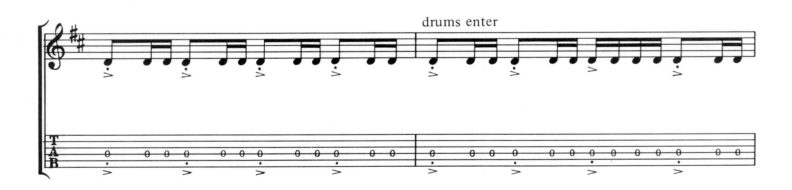

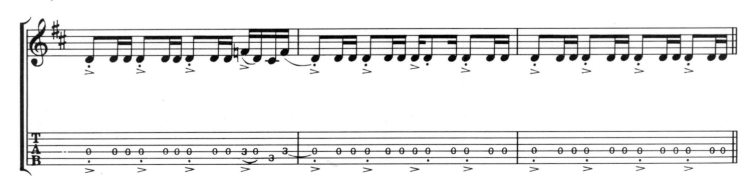

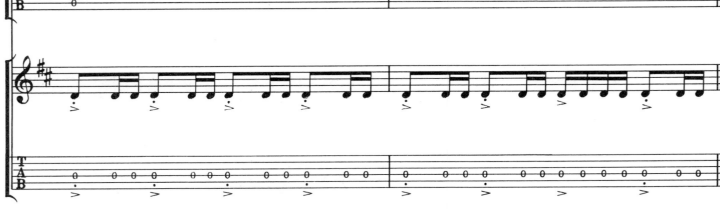

make your **face** up with your fa - vor - ite — dis - guise — with your
run all day and run all — night — and

*synthesizer solo on %

Fmaj9♭5

but - ton down lips and your roll - er blind — eyes, — with your
keep your dir - ty feel - ings your deep in — side, — and if you're

run.

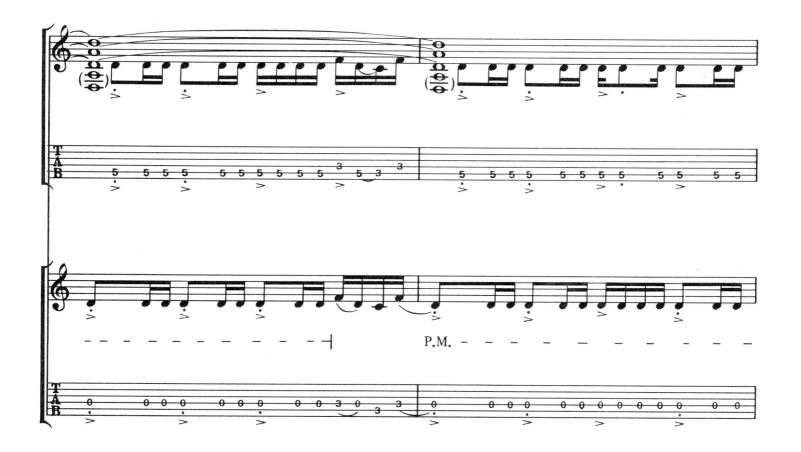

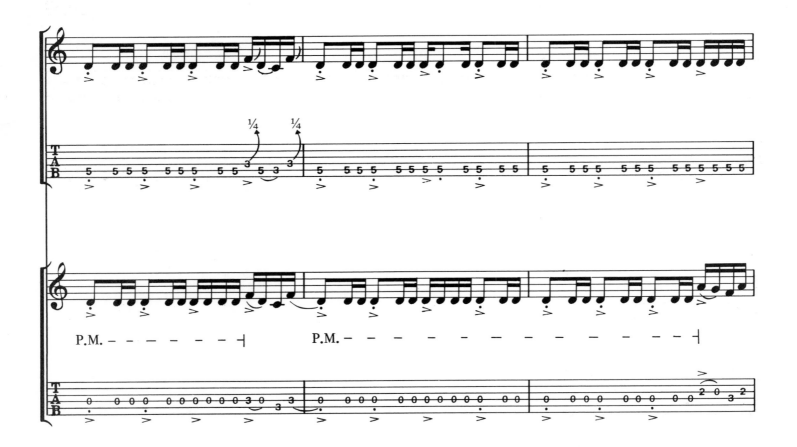

with Fill 1

Fill 1

Words & Music by
ROGER WATERS

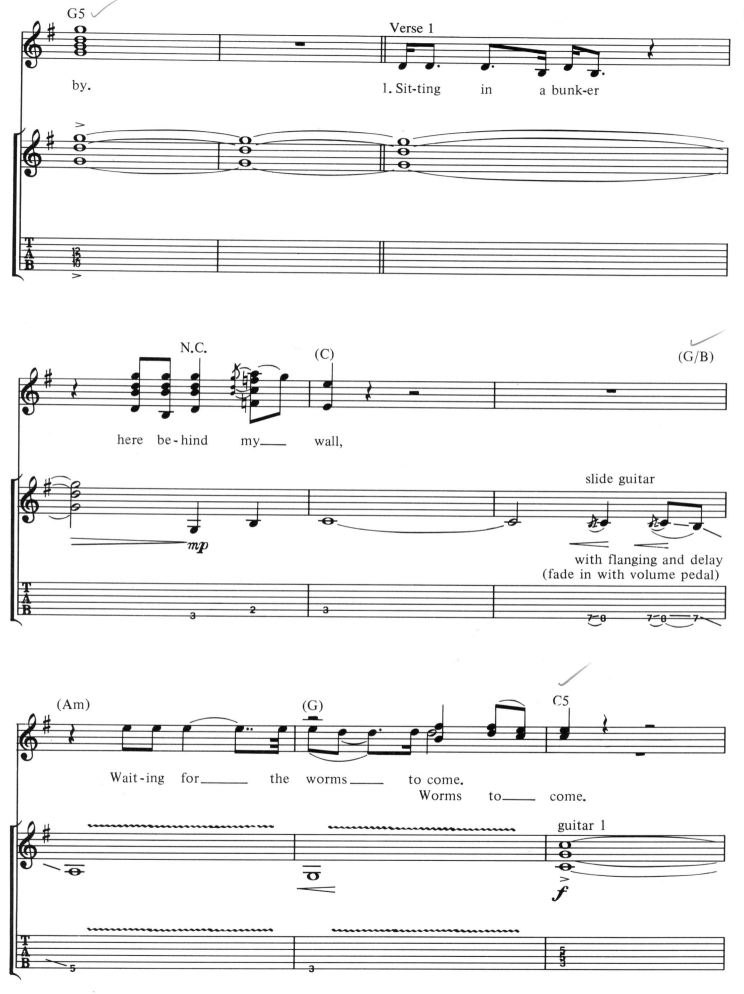

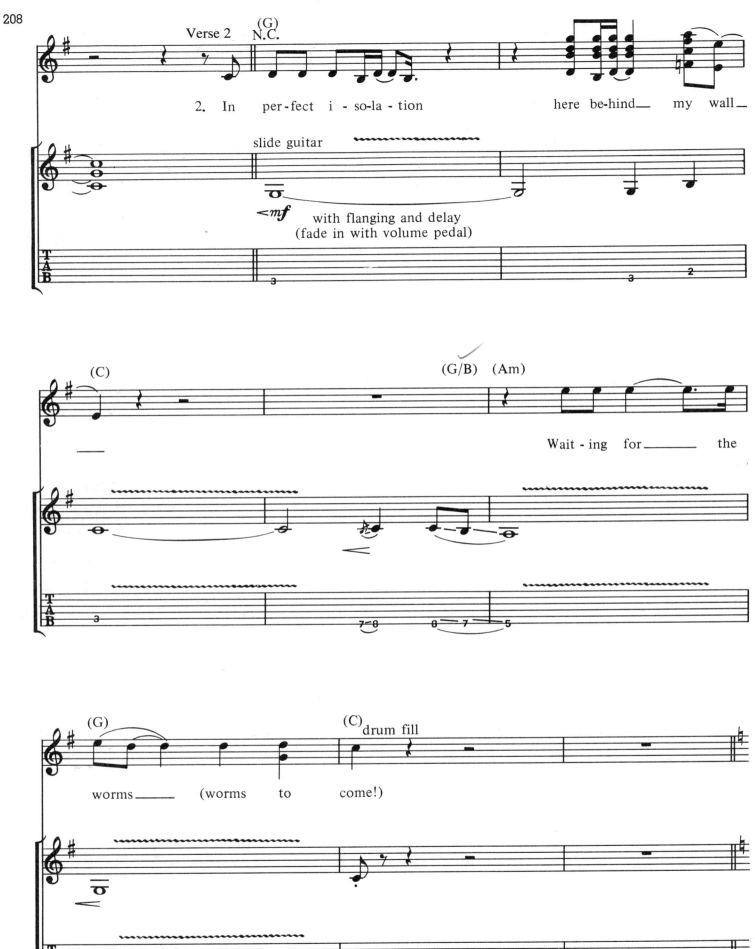

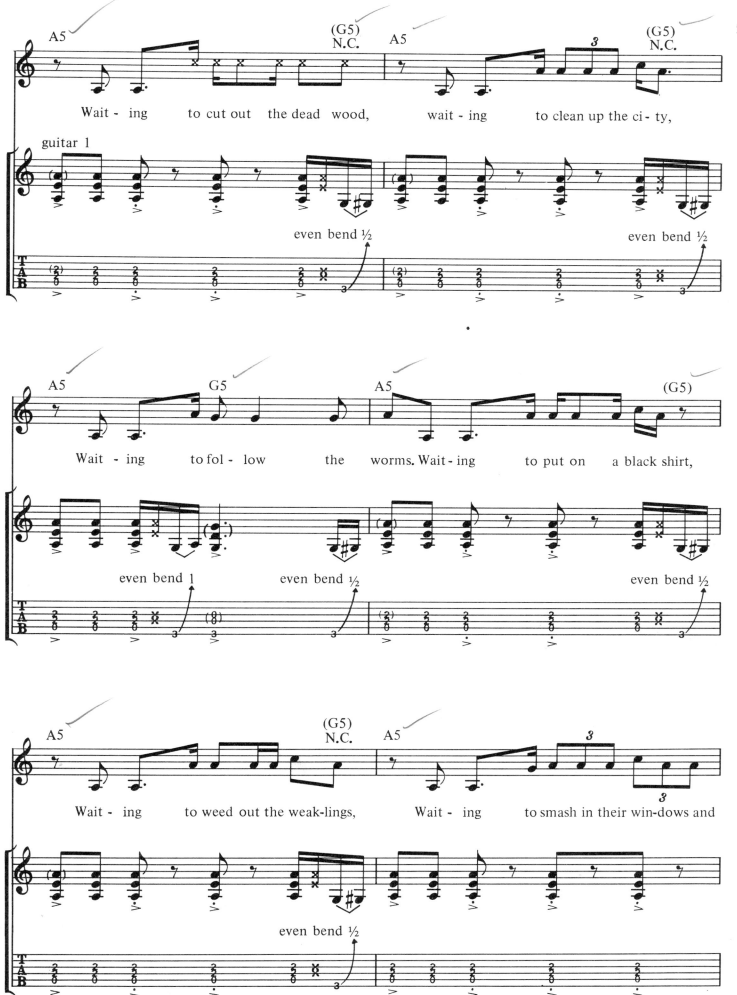

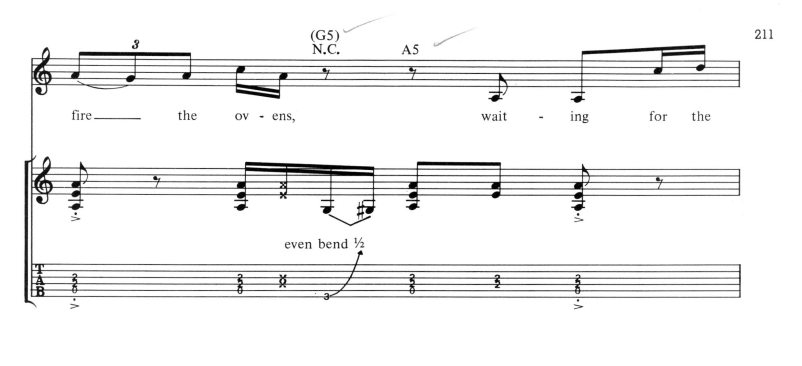

fire _____ the ov - ens, wait - ing for the

even bend ½

queens and the coons and the reds and the Jews.

even bend ½

Wait - ing to fol - low _____ the worms. ___

even bend

even bend

Would you like to see＿＿＿＿ Bri - tan-nia rule＿＿＿＿ a - gain＿＿＿

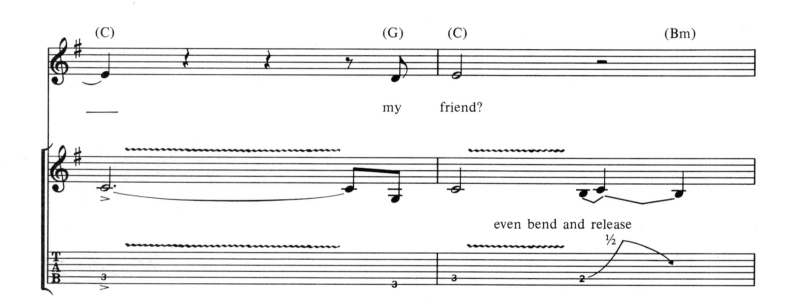

my friend?

even bend and release

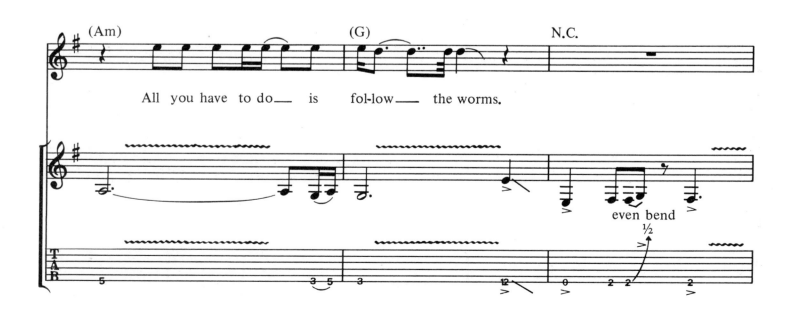

All you have to do＿ is fol-low＿ the worms.

even bend

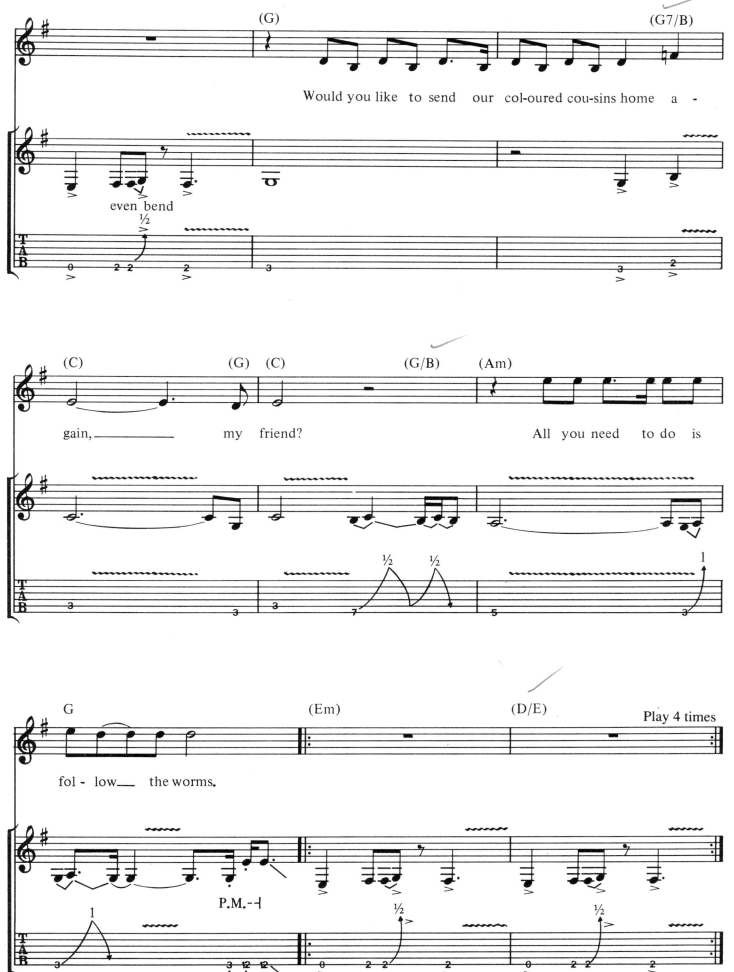

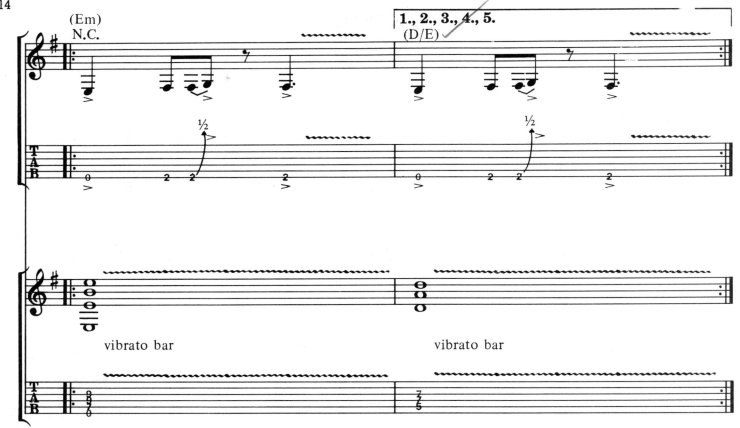

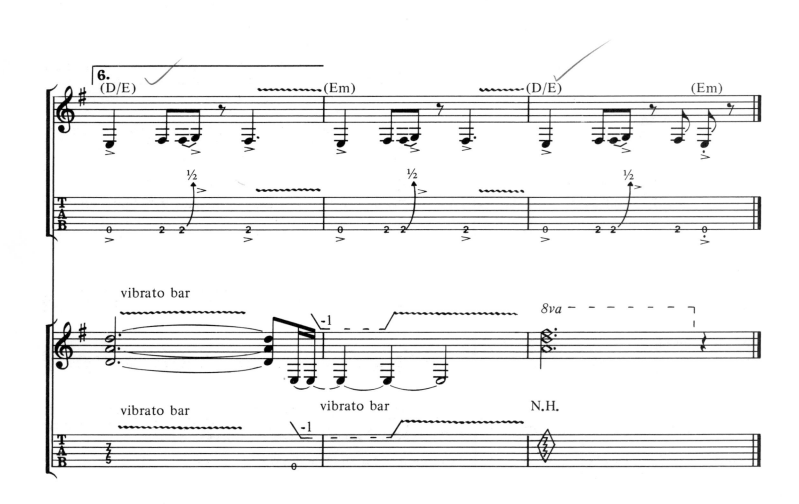

Stop

Words & Music by
ROGER WATERS

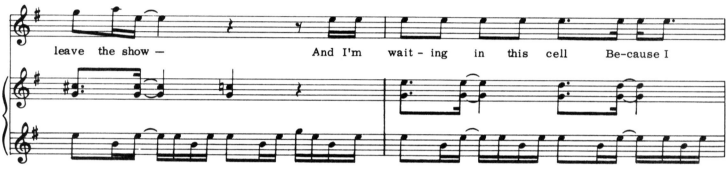

The Trial

Words by ROGER WATERS
Music by ROGER WATERS/BOB EZRIN

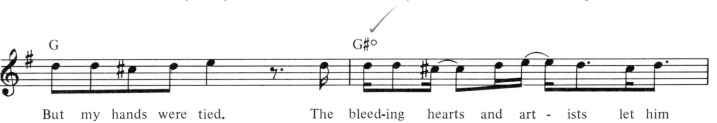

get in an-y trou-ble, why'd he ev-er have to leave___ me? Worm, your

hon-our, let me take him home.___ Cra - zy, ov-er the rain - bow, I am

cra - zy, bars in the win - dow. There

must have been a door___ there in the wall, ___ When I came

children's in.
choir: Cra - zy o - ver the rain - bow he is cra - zy.

This ev-i-dence___ be-fore___ the court ___ is in-con-tro-vert-i-ble, there's

electric guitars 1 and 2

_f_ with distortion

no need for the ju - ry to re - tire.___ In all___

___ my years of judg - ing, I have nev - er heard be - fore___ of

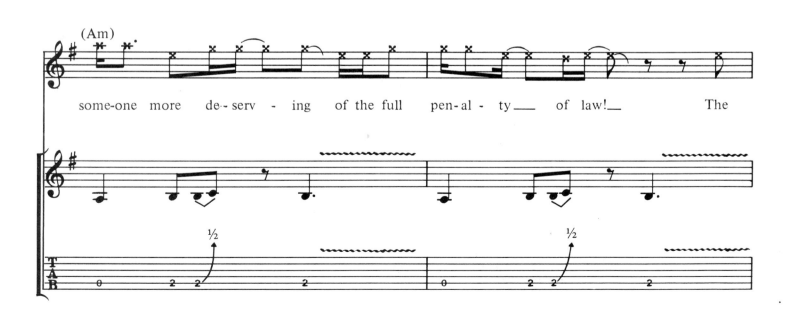

some - one more de - serv - ing of the full pen - al - ty___ of law!___ The

way you made them suf-fer, your ex - qui-site wife and moth-er,

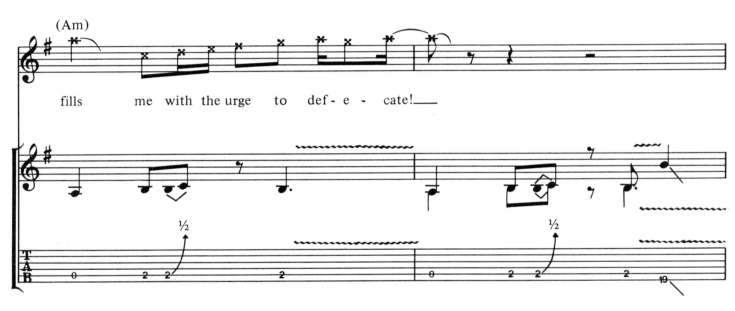

fills me with the urge to def-e-cate!___

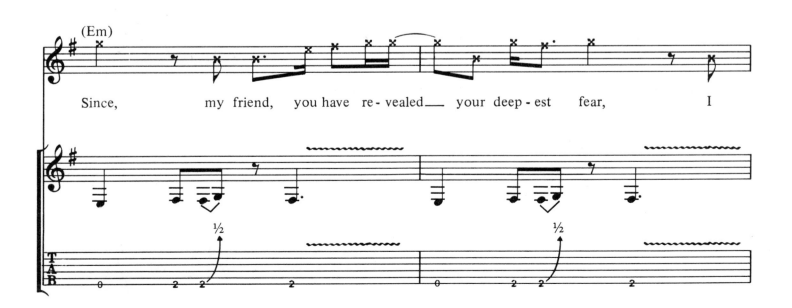

Since, my friend, you have re-vealed___ your deep-est fear, I

(Am) ... (Em)

sen - tence you to be— ex -posed be - fore your peers! Tear down— the wall!

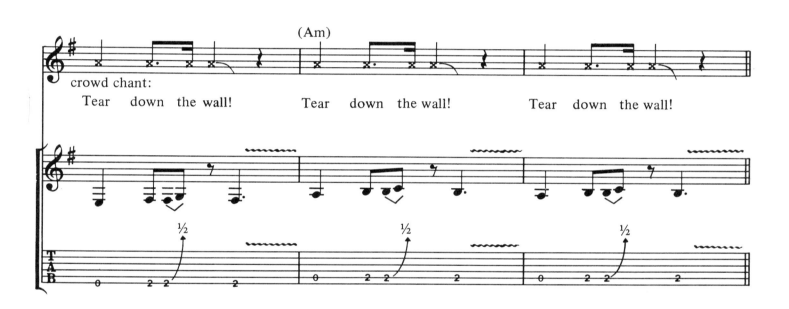

(Am)

crowd chant:

Tear down the wall! Tear down the wall! Tear down the wall!

(Em) (Am)

repeat and fade
(with explosive sound effects)

Tear down the wall! Tear down the wall! Tear down the wall! Tear down the wall!

Outside the Wall

Words & Music by
ROGER WATERS

hand,_____ And some gath - ered to - geth - er in bands,_____ The

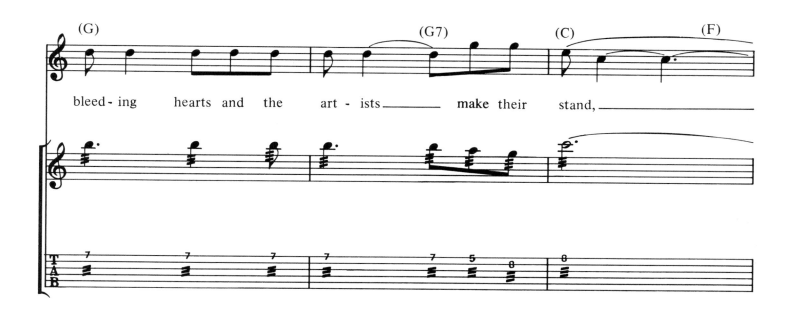

bleed - ing hearts and the art - ists_____ **make** their stand,_____

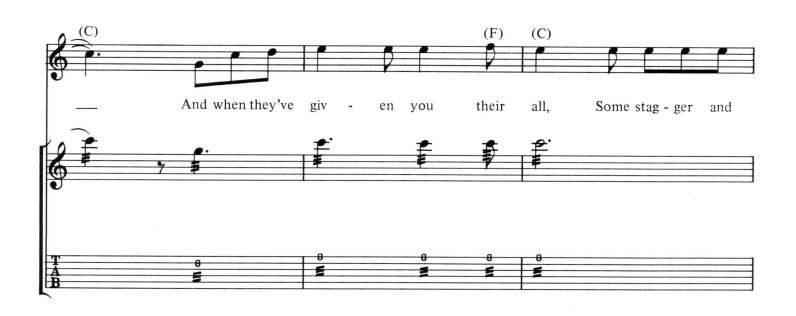

— And when they've giv - en you their all, Some stag - ger and

fall. Aft-er all it's not ea-sy,_____ Bang-ing your heart a-gainst

some mad bug-ger's Wall._____

a tempo

Spoken: "Isn't this where..?"

**Published by Pink Floyd Music Publishers Ltd.,
27 Noel Street, London W1V 3RD.**

Exclusive Distributors:
Music Sales Corporation
225 Park Avenue South, New York, NY 10003
Music Sales Limited
8/9 Frith Street, London W1V 5TZ England
Music Sales Pty. Limited
120 Rothschild Street, Rosebery, Sydney, NSW 2018, Australia

Transcribed by Jesse Gress
Printed in the United States of America by
Vicks Lithograph and Printing Corporation